Buddhist Abhidhamma
Meditation and Concentration

Buddhist Abhidhamma
Meditation and Concentration

U KYAW MIN

HEIAN

FIRST AMERICAN EDITION, 1987
Not for sale outside U. S. A.

HEIAN INTERNATIONAL
P.O. Box 1013
Union City, CA 94587 USA.

First published in Singapore by
Times Books International
Times Centre, 1 New Industrial Road
Singapore 1953

© **1980 TIMES BOOKS INTERNATIONAL**, Singapore

Reprinted January 1984

All rights reserved. No part of this publication may be reproduced, stored in a retrieval system, or transmitted, in any form or by any means, electronic, mechanical, photocopying, recording or otherwise, without the prior permission of the publisher.

ISBN: 0-89346-287-X

Printed in Singapore.

Dedication

This book is gratefully dedicated to my two Teachers,

1. The Revd. U Nagasena, who was formerly Saya U Ba Gyaw.

2. U Thein Nyun, who assisted U Narada (Mula Patthana Sayadaw) in the translation of **Dathukatha** (Discourse on Elements) and **Patthana** (Conditional Relations), being the third and seventh Treatises of the Abhidhamma. He is the Author of many articles on Buddhism, such as, 'Approach to Practical Buddhism', 'The 4 Noble Truths', 'Mind the Mind'.

Contents

BOOK I
BUDDHIST ABHIDHAMMA
Part One: ABHIDHAMMA

Introduction
Chapter 1 —	Preliminaries	·5
Chapter 2 —	Consciousness	21
Chapter 3 —	The 5-Aggregates	32
Chapter 4 —	Mind and Matter	42
Chapter 5 —	The 4 Noble Truths	52

Part Two: MEDITATION

Chapter 6 —	Right Understanding	68
Chapter 7 —	Vipassana Meditation	77

BOOK II
CONCENTRATION

Introduction
Chapter 1 —	Your Mind	96
Chapter 2 —	Consciousness	101
Chapter 3 —	The Superconscious Mind	104
Chapter 4 —	Preliminary Concentration Exercises	107

Chapter 5 —	Buddhist Method of Mental Culture	114
Chapter 6 —	Ana-Pana, or Mindfulness of Breathing	117
Chapter 7 —	Jhāna Concentration	121
Chapter 8 —	Walking on Water	128
Chapter 9 —	Concentration on Loving Kindness	132

BOOK III
SOME AUTO-SUGGESTIONS

Chapter 1 —	Breathing	137
Chapter 2 —	Sleep and Insomnia	141
Chapter 3 —	Auto-Suggestion	146
Chapter 4 —	Absent-Mindedness	149
Chapter 5 —	Basic Good Conduct	154
Chapter 6 —	Self-Healing	158

APPENDICES

I	Materiality	160
II	Cetasikas	162
III	Abhidhamma	171
Pali Equivalents		174
INDEX		181

Book I

Buddhist Abhidhamma

Introduction

Abhidhamma is the 3rd or last Basket of the Buddhist Scriptures. It is said to be abstruse, profound and subtle. It has been described as a Valley of Dry Bones. This book is an attempt to put some flesh on the dry bones and may be regarded as a Manual introducing Abhidhamma. (Abhidharma)
During the few weeks directly after his Enlightenment, the Buddha intuitively acquired the Abhidhamma and it is therefore about the earliest product of his thought. This is conclusively proved by the internal evidence of the first two Sermons which he preached to his former 5 Companions, called the 5 Vaggi. The first Sermon is called the Discourse setting the Wheel of the Doctrine in motion. The second is the Anatta-Lakkhana Sutta, called the Discourse on the characteristics of Anatta.
In the first Discourse, he was telling the 5 Vaggi why he can declare that he was the Buddha, the Enlightened. They refused to listen to him at first. The Sermon lasted 5 days but it is very concisely adumbrated into 2½ pages. In this Sermon, the Buddha explained that the 5 constituent groups of existence, which are the objects of clinging, are Suffering; this is Abhidhamma, which in this book has been called the 5 Aggregates and clinging Aggregate.
The Second Sermon is purely Abhidhamma, dealing as it does, with corporeality, sensation, perception, kamma-activities and consciousness, and the 11 different distinctions of each Aggregate.

However, legend has it that it would be necessary to expound the Abhidhamma in one sitting, and as it would take 3 whole months in human time, this was impossible in the human world. It was 7 years after his Enlightenment, during the 3 months of Lent, that he went up to the world of the Devas where his former mother was reborn, and taught the Abhidhamma non-stop. Every day, however, he took time off for his food, and left a Buddha after his own image, conjured up by his miraculous power, to carry on his good work. He also taught his Chief Disciple Sariputta, who had a marvellous mind. It was Sariputta who taught the Abhidhamma to his 500 Disciples.

Abhidhamma now forms the third Basket of the Scriptures, and consists of 7 treatises. The last is the Patthana, also called the Big Book which alone takes up 5 voluminous sections.

The reader must supplement his knowledge of Buddhism by reading the books written in conventional terms. But it is only by a knowledge of the Abhidhamma that even the Discourses of the Buddha, embodied in the Second Basket of the Scriptures, can be understood in their full and proper meaning.

The ideas about ultimate reality form the background of Insight Meditation. Insight Meditation leads to Path Wisdom and to Nirvana, which is our Goal. Everything else is a waste of valuable time.

The following is an excerpt from the Expositor I. p.37: 'And tradition has it that those bhikkhus only who know Abhidhamma are true preachers of Dhamma; the rest, though they speak on the Dhamma, are not preachers thereof. And why? They, in speaking on the Dhamma, confuse the different kinds of kamma and of its results, the distinction between mind and matter, and the different kinds of states (dhammas). The students of Abhidhamma do not thus get confused: hence a bhikkhu who knows Abhidhamma, whether he preaches the Dhamma or not, will be able to answer questions whenever asked. He alone, therefore, is a true preacher of the Dhamma.'

If there are any misleading statements in this book, the responsibility is solely mine.

Part One
Abhidhamma

Chapter 1

Preliminaries

1. The Future Buddha

Prince Siddartha was the eldest son of King Suddhodhana. His mother was Queen Mahamaya, and on the night he was conceived, she had a wonderful dream. She related the dream to her royal husband, who summoned the Sage Asita to explain its meaning. He told the royal parents that the Queen had conceived a son who would one day become either a Universal Monarch or a Buddha.

The King wanted his son to become a Universal Monarch and did not like the idea of his son becoming a Buddha. With that aim, he surrounded his son with sensual pleasures.

Prince Siddartha was married to Princess Yasodhara. He was given 3 palaces to suit the 3 seasons. One day, whilst he was driving through the Park, he saw an aged person. On another occasion he saw a diseased person, and later a corpse.

All this is described in the Anguttara-Nikaya, III, 35, as 'Warnings' regarding decay, disease, and death, and has been put in a rhetorical way.

Herewith:

Did you never see in the world a man, or a woman, eighty, or ninety, or a hundred years old, frail, crooked as a gable-roof, bent down, resting on crutches, with tottering steps, infirm, youth long since fled, with broken teeth, grey and scanty hair, or bald-headed, wrinkled, with blotched limbs? And did the thought never come to you that also you are subject to decay, that you cannot escape it?

Did you never see in the world a man, or a woman, who, being sick, afflicted, and grievously ill, and wallowing in their filth, was lifted up by some people, and put to bed by others? And did the thought never come to you that also you are subject to disease, and also you cannot escape it?

Did you never see in the world the corpse of a man, or a woman, one or two or three days after death, swollen-up, blue black in colour, and full of corruption? And did the thought never come to you that also you are subject to death, and that also you cannot escape it?

What he saw and the explanations he received no doubt made a great impression on this introspective young man.

At the age of 29, on the birth of a child, he renounced his kingdom, for the purpose of solving the riddle of birth and death.

For fully 6 years, he studied under the Greatest Teachers of the day, meditating, or what would be called concentrating his mind. Finally, along with 5 companions, called the 5 Vaggi, he took to ascetic practices and achieved all the psychic powers that could be got.

He had obtained the 5 super-intellections, one of which was the seeing of past existences. He was a Hindu and had the preconceived idea that what he saw were the souls of the different beings transmigrating from existence to existence.

One day he fell down in a swoon for lack of strength. On his recovery he realised that he was not getting to the bottom of what he renounced his kingdom to find out, namely the problem of birth and death.

He began to eat again and finally on the full-moon eve of May he sat down under the Bodhi tree to meditate. The time was now ripe for him to distinguish between ultimate realities and conventional concepts and ideas.

It was only by meditating on ultimate realities that he came to realise the illusions and delusions and hallucinations and perversions induced by Mind-consciousness, allegorised as Mara, the King of Darkness, whom I have called the Great Magician.

The Buddha achieved Enlightenment at the dawn of the next day.

He now understood that there was no transmigration of souls but results of deeds which bring about beings from one existence to another.

2. Ultimates

Water exists. However, a molecule of water can be subdivided into H_2O, namely, two atoms of hydrogen to one atom of oxygen; therefore, water, as such, cannot be regarded as an ultimate, for an ultimate, by definition, is something that cannot be subdivided.

Once again, an atom is not an ultimate unit, for it can be subdivided into protons, electrons and neutrons. These protons, electrons and neutrons are not ultimates either, for they can be subdivided into atomic particles and muons and quarks, and may be these are the present ultimates in science.

There are two kinds of truth, one is conventional truth, like our concept of water, and there is ultimate truth, like atomic particles.

This book deals with ultimate realities in Buddhism. You cannot see an ultimate with the naked eye but only with the eye of wisdom, that can be called the "inner eye". Similarly, you cannot see an atom or a molecule except with the "inner eye".

Just pause for a moment to consider that the whole body of water in this universe, the lakes and rivers and oceans are not ultimates; they exist only in conventional language but they do not exist in terms of ultimates.

There are ultimates in Matter (materiality) and ultimates in Mind (mentality), and they are seen by the Buddhist inner eye as having or manifesting properties or qualities. But nothing exists apart from the ultimates.

Each of these ultimates has its individual essence, or intrinsic nature. One has to come to realise these individual essences by contemplation or meditation, both the individual essences of the ultimates in Matter and ultimates in Mind.

Mind and Matter can be likened to a Cripple and a Blind Man. The Cripple cannot walk, and the Blind man cannot see. When the cripple is put on the shoulders of the blind man, the cripple can see and directs the blind man to go left and right.

Mind wants to eat but it cannot eat, and it is the body that eats. Mind wants to drink, but it cannot drink and it is the body that drinks. It is the Mind that controls and directs.

The categories of the ultimate realities in Buddhism are:
1. Consciousness,
2. Mind Constituents,
3. Materiality,
4. Nirvana.

3. Ultimates in Matter

The ultimates in Matter are 28, namely,
a. The 4 essential qualities or properties of
   1. hardness, or softness;
   2. cohesion or fluidity;
   3. heat or lack of heat; and
   4. motion or resistance to motion.
b. The 4 secondary qualities or properties of
   1. colour
   2. smell
   3. taste
   4. nutriment

These eight properties are inseparable and are called the Octad. They are explained more fully later, and also how to see each property or quality with the inner eye. The other 20 properties are listed in the Appendix.

We have mentioned the ultimates in Matter.

Matter is generated by:
1. Karma
2. Mind
3. Temperature
4. Nutriment

They are called
1. Karma-produced matter
2. Mind-produced matter
3. Temperature-produced matter, and
4. Nutriment-produced matter

Matter is being produced all the time by these 4 causes. At any instant, the karma-produced matter may be prominent, at other times Mind-produced matter may be prominent or temperature-produced matter or nutriment-produced matter.

It must be remembered that these ultimate realities in matter are what can be visualised only by the inner eye. But the properties or qualities are reflected in the human body. When you are angry, even a child can sense that you are angry. Similarly for other emotions; your body will reflect your emotions and moods.

4. Consciousness

There are 5 sense-organs in the body, and if anyone is defective, for instance, if you are blind or deaf, people are not apt to accept you as a full human being. The body has no sentience.

You see something. There arises visual consciousness.
You hear something. There arises auditory consciousness.

You smell something. There arises smell or olfactory consciousness.
You taste something. There arises gustatory consciousness.
You touch something. There arises tactile consciousness.

You day-dream or think of something, without the basis of any of the 5 senses. There arises ideational consciousness, or Mind-Consciousness.

It is the function of the eye to see, the ear to hear, and the nose to smell, etc. The eye cannot hear or smell, and the ear cannot see or smell, and the nose cannot see or hear, etc.

Consciousness arises and disappears immediately. Only one consciousness can arise at a time and it immediately disappears for the next consciousness to arise.

5. Mental Constituents

Mind is consciousness plus something. Along with any consciousness, there arise certain mental constituents like love, hate, anger, disgust, disappointment, etc. These mental constituents are also translated as mental factors, mental concomitants, mental adjuncts, psychic factors, etc.

There are 52 mental constituents. When any consciousness arises, some appropriate mental constituents always arise. These mental constituents arise and disappear along with consciousness.

Some 7 mental constituents always arise with every unit of consciousness and they are called universals. Some 6 others arise as a whole or in parts. The remainder are morally good or bad or neutral and they arise in different combinations.

When a consciousness disappears, all the mental constituents that have arisen along with it also disappear simultaneously.

Each mental constituent has its own individual essence. For example the individual essences of the 7 universals are:

1. Contact
2. Feeling

3. Perception
4. Volition
5. One-pointedness of Mind
6. Psychic Life
7. Attention

Consciousness is extremely swift. Commentators say that in the time taken by the twinkling of an eye or a flash of lightning, there are more than a billion consciousnesses. We can paraphrase it by saying that a consciousness takes about a billionth of a second to function.

In a course-of-cognition, which is called a thought-process by certain authors, there are 17 thought-moments. In each thought-moment there are three phases, namely arising, development and cessation.

A thought-process always follows a certain sequence of consciousnesses; it is explained in more detail in the next chapter.

We receive information of the outside world through 5 sense-doors. There is also a sixth door, called Mind-door, through which we cognise our own ideas; this is mind consciousness, by which we imagine.

So far as a material object is concerned, it exists for 17 thought-moments till a new material object takes its place and exists for 17 thought-moments.

6. Conventional Truth

You were told the distinction between ultimate truth and conventional truth. This conventional or relative truth is also called concepts, ideas, notions, names or terms.

A concept either makes known or is made known.

The different kinds are given different names. There are collective concepts, general concepts, derivative concepts, formal concepts, concepts relating to locality, time and space, concepts of nothingness, and continuity, and conceptualised after-images (in concentration) and conventional signs.

11

Some may be interested in the Pali names: **Santhana pannatti** are concepts of form, like land, mountains, etc.

Samuha pannatti are collective concepts, corresponding to a collection or group of things, like chariot, table.

Disa pannatti refer to concepts of locality.

Kala pannatti refer to concepts of time.

Akasa pannatti refer to space, like caves, wells.

Nimitta pannatti refer to conceptualised images, visualised images.

7. Ultimates

The ultimates are:

1.	Consciousness	1
2.	Mind constituents	52
3.	Nirvana	1
4.	Matter	28
		82 ultimates

All that is not an ultimate can be called a concept.

This distinction between ultimate and concept is important. An ultimate exists in reality. It is the bedrock of all existence; they are the ultimates in matter and mind. They really exist, and what does not really exist is said not to exist. So such things as lakes, rivers, mountains, a human being, a person, a male, a female, do not exist in reality and are said not to exist. They are concepts. It is called spoken or relative truth. They are just words and ideas and names, and are therefore conventional truth. They are not ultimate reality.

It was only under the Bodhi-Tree that the future-Buddha came to understand the difference between ultimates and concepts. Previously, his world was the world of concepts; now it was the world of ultimates. Only on meditation on ultimates did he achieve Enlightenment. Similarly you must meditate on ultimates in Insight Meditation.

8. Subject and Object

In Abhidhamma, there is always a subject and an object, and they arise together simultaneously.

The subject is 'I' in conceptual language. The object can be anything at all. In terms of ultimates, the subject is consciousness, mental constituent and matter. When we turn the mind inwards and think of the immediately past mind, the subject becomes the object.

Mind is consciousness plus a few appropriate mental constituents. When we speak of mind, we can also say consciousness.

The objects taken by the different minds are either one of the 5 sense objects or an ideational object. Mind is also regarded in Buddhism as one of the senses, making 6 senses in all. Consciousness can get more and more exalted till it reaches the very heights. How exalted can your consciousness become? It cannot get very exalted if it is bogged down by immoral or evil thoughts or what is called craving or selfish desire or thirst. You will hear more about this craving.

9. Three Spheres or Realms

In the universe, there are 3 Spheres or Realms, namely,
1. Sphere or Realm of sensuous desire
2. Sphere or Realm of Form
3. Sphere or Realm of the Formless

In the sphere of sensuous desires, there are morally good and morally bad consciousness and the neutral. Unless you have transcended your bad thoughts and inclinations, your consciousness cannot reach the sphere of Form and the Formless, where the consciousnesses are all good.

It is the function of mental development to get your consciousness more and more exalted. Eventually there is Nirvana (Nibbana) which can be attained if craving is permanently eliminated.

By Insight Meditation, by methods of acquiring the required Wisdom, Nirvana ia attained. Buddhism is the only religion that promises its Goal or **summum bonum** during your life time and you do not have to wait till after death.

10. 31 Planes of Existence

In this Universe, we talk of the "human world", the "animal world", the "plant world", etc., but we do not think of them as different material worlds or different places.

There are 31 planes of existence. The human mind can descend to the lowest depths and also ascend to the highest regions. We reach the heights as the result of the states of concentration called Zen.

The Realm of sensuous desire is divided into 6 main planes according to their respective degrees of suffering. They are in ascending order:

1. The plane of Purgatory
2. The plane of animals
3. The plane of beings in whom the desire outweighs the possibilities of satisfaction (Peta)
4. The plane of ghosts
5. The human plane
6. The 6 planes of Higher Beings within the sense world

The 4 lower planes are called the abodes of misery.

The two higher ones, including the human plane, are the abodes of fortunate sense-experience.

In the Realm of Pure Form, the only senses are the visual, the aural (auditory), and the mental.

The intensity of consciousness, namely, in purity and in its light, increases. Here, we have Beings of radiant light, or limited or boundless aura, limited or infinite radiance, and Beings of the abodes of purity.

The description of the 4 Planes of non-Form coincides with that of the 4 Stages of non-Form consciousness.

The human Mind can reach all these Planes by practising the methods for reaching them. The human Mind can attain all the Zen consciousnesses as the result of which beings are reborn in all the higher planes.

11. Death and Rebirth

The death consciousness of this existence occurs at the end of the dying process. The next consciousness is the Rebirth-linking consciousness, which is the moment of conception in the next existence.

It is explained in the Patthana, the last book of the Abhidhamma, that when death ceases, the force of proximity condition brings about the next consciousness which is the Rebirth-Linking Consciousness. It is further explained that the force left behind produces results. Although an asynchronous faultless or faulty volition arises for one thought-moment and then ceases, this is not the end of it. For a special force is left behind in the mind's successive continuity so that at some time in the future, the appropriate result of that volition will be produced when the proper conditions are satisfied. It is due to the presence of this force that results appear. However, this force does not manifest itself like the mind with its nascent, static and cessant phases but is present like the latent tendencies. And just as the latter are not concepts, so also this special force of asynchronous kamma is not a concept. It is a special force of the ultimate realities. It may be called a germinal force.

The Rebirth-Linking consciousness lasts for one thought-moment only and is then called the undercurrent subconsciousness which lasts for 16 thought-moments impelled by its craving for existence and then sinks into the passive state of mind.

It is at the moment of conception that the foetus gets its tactile sense organ and the heart-basis, and its gender, whether it is going to be a male or a female, and all these are produced by its past karma.

At the end of each course-of-cognition, the undercurrent subconsciousnesses arise and cease successively till the next course-of-cognition occurs. But consciousnesses are so swift that the undercurrent subconsciousnesses in between are not detectable. How many thought-moments your undercurrent subconscious takes between courses-of-cognition depends on the stage of your mind-development. It is the aim of mind-development to reduce the time of the undercurrent subconscious, and the shorter the time, the more alert is your mind. It determines the acuteness of your brain.

This death consciousness takes as its object one of the three things. At the last moment, the person thinks of something that has been most prominent in his mind. A murderer may get an idea that he is going to commit a crime, whereas a pious man may think he is worshipping the Buddha or listening to a sermon. This is known as the 'vision of action'.

Or he may see an article generally associated with his action. The murderer may see a knife whilst the pious man may see a yellow robe. This is the 'vision of an article associated with the action'.

Or he may get a vision of hell-fire or a vision of the higher regions. This is known as the 'vision of the sign of destiny'.

Your undercurrent subconscious of this existence has as its object what was the object of your last dying-process.

After each course-of-cognition, the mind goes back to the undercurrent subconscious.

Life has been compared to a river which has its beginning or source at birth and its mouth at death (cuti). It seems to have a constant form or identity but there is not a drop today of all the water that composed it yesterday.

This stream of life or being is also called the life-continuum by certain authors; it is the passive state of mind as in dreamless sleep.

The dividing line between Being and Thought is called the Mind Door; it is the threshold of consciousness. Below the threshold is subliminal consciousness, and above the threshold is supraliminal consciousness.

One Indian author is of the opinion that a thought may be compared to a wave in the sea. The wave rises up from the surface and then sinks down again. Similarly, a thought rises up from the surface of the undercurrent subconscious and sinks back to its base; it sinks back between courses-of-cognition and after cognition is over before the start of any new course-of-cognition. However, this opinion is not universally accepted as it is said that the undercurrent subconscious is arrested before a thought commences.

For a vivid sense-object, there are 17 thought-moments in a course-of-cognition, after which the undercurrent subconsciousnesses arise and cease successively for a few hundred thought-moments and then there arises the second course-of cognition, followed by a few hundred more undercurrent subconsciousnesses.

Then there are thousands and thousands of more impressions, and courses-of-cognition, each followed at the end of each course by undercurrent subconsciousnesses the durations of which are about 30,000 or 40,000 thought-moments. It is said that chief Disciple Sariputta had such a great mind that there were only a few hundred undercurrent subconsciousnesses after each course-of-cognition.

It is the function of mind development to reduce the duration of the undercurrent sub-consciousnesses between the course-of-cognition. The quick mind has only a few thousand undercurrent sub-consciousnesses after each course-of-cognition.

You cannot be born a human being without some good karma in the sum total of previous existences. Nevertheless ignorance and craving of which you will hear a lot later, are pulling, like gravity, to bad deeds, to blindness of moral vision. Your education during all your childhood years, including your training, makes you a better and better person changing your blindness to a better vision. The time will come when you will be more good than bad. Or, if you cannot profit from your education, you will be predominantly bad.

12. Subjective Mind

All verbal and physical actions are motivated by the mind. If you raise your hand or you sit down or you walk, it is all mind-motivated action.

It is well known that old people cannot hear certain sounds that are audible to younger people. And certain sounds heard by animals cannot be heard by humans. It does not mean, however, that these sounds do not exist.

Moreover, if the Mind is absorbed in something also and attention is not paid to these sounds, the Mind does not hear these sounds. In these cases, the sounds do not exist for the Mind.

Only when the Mind takes these sounds as objects can they be heard by a person, and they exist for the Mind.

Things may exist in the world but they are not known to the Mind, if they are not objects of the Mind.

However, the Mind cannot take everything as objects at one and the same time. The Mind can take as an object only one thing at any one time, and the rest of the world is non-existent so far as the Mind is concerned.

The Minds that have already disappeared are no more existent, and the Minds that are yet born are still non-existent. Mind consciousness exists at the present moment only, though the object it takes can be of the past, present or future, real or imaginary.

13. Noble Ones

There are 4 types of individuals, called the Noble Ones, who are near the Goal:

1. 'the one who has entered the stream'
2. 'the once-returner'
3. 'the non-returner'
4. 'the Holy One' (Arahat), who has realized the Summum Bonum.

A definition of these Noble Ones is found in the fourth book of the Abhidhamma-Pitaka 26-27:

He who has overcome the three fetters; such a man is called 'one who has entered the stream'.

He in whom sensual desire and anger are utterly reduced; such a man is called 'once-returner'.

He who has completely overcome sensual desire and anger; such a man is called 'non-returner'.

He who has completely overcome the craving for the world of Pure Form or of Non-Form as well as pride, restlessness, and ignorance; such a man is called a "Holy One".

Of the ten fetters by which the ordinary human being is bound to the world, the 'stream enterer' has overcome the first three:

1. the belief in a permanent personality
2. doubt (or scepticism)
3. clinging to rules and rituals

The remaining seven fetters are:
4. sensual desire
5. aversion or anger;
6. craving for existence in the world of Pure Form
7. craving for existence in the world of Non-Form
8. pride
9. restlessness
10. ignorance, delusion

The first five are called the lower fetters. The five higher fetters are only overcome by the arahat. Here is a short summary:

ARIYA-PUGALA		SAMYOJANANI
I	Stream-entrant	1-3
II	Once-returner	1-3; 4 and 5 partly
III	Non-returner	1-5
IV	Arahat or Holy one	1-10

14. Mundane and Supramundane Wisdom

The whole world is using mundane wisdom.

All Western philosophers are using mundane wisdom. But there is another wisdom, called the Supra-mundane Wisdom. This Book will explain how you become a Noble One. Say, you meet a pretty girl who wants to come and live with you. On making enquiries, you learn that she has the dose, and that she tells lies and she is a habitual thief. You use mundane wisdom to decide that she will cause you suffering, and you turn down the proposition.

The other Wisdom is called Insight Wisdom leading to Path Wisdom which leads to Nirvana, our Summum Bonum. It is also called Transcendental or Supramundane Wisdom.

Chapter 2

Consciousness

How does a consciousness arise? It arises through one of the five sense-doors and also through the mind-door.

When a material thing like the "sensitive" eye takes as object a material thing called the visual object, there arises visual consciousness. When the conditions are fulfilled, nothing in the world can stop the visual consciousness from arising. The conditions are that there should be an eye base and a visual object and light and attention. In other words, if the eye were non-existent as, for example, in the case of a blind man, there can be no visual consciousness. If there is no light, and there is complete darkness, the visual consciousness cannot arise. So also, there must be attention. With so many competing stimuli, which may be a visual stimulus or an auditory stimulus or any of the five sense stimuli, whichever catches the attention of the mind, produces the corresponding sense consciousness.

Similarly, for an auditory consciousness to arise, there must be an ear-base, the appropriate sound waves and the medium of air (any suitable medium) and attention. If the ear organ were non-existent, as in the case of a deaf person, there cannot be an auditory consciousness. There must be the medium for the sound waves to travel and the waves must be within the frequency range for that particular ear. Once again, attention is a **sine qua non**.

Similarly, for an olfactory consciousness to arise, there must be the nose organ, the smell stimulus, and the medium of air and, of course, attention.

Similarly for a taste consciousness to arise, there must be the tongue organ and the object that is tasted, and the saliva as the medium, and attention.

Similarly for the touch or tactile consciousness to arise, there must be present the sensitive part of the body and the object that is felt and the medium to convey the sense, and attention. Sometimes the sense of touch is defective or has deteroriated and people have been burnt because of the lack of the sense of touch.

It will be seen that the mental factor of attention must always be present.

The following Table shows how the Consciousnesses arise:

Six Sense Organs
1. Eye
2. Ear
3. Nose
4. Tongue
5. Body
6. Mind Element

Six Sense Objects
1. Visible object
2. Sound object
3. Smell object
4. Taste object
5. Tangible object
6. Mental object

Six Consciousnesses
1. Visual consciousness
2. Auditory consciousness
3. Nasal consciousness
4. Gustatory consciousness
5. Tactile consciousness
6. Mind-consciousness

Note:

The Mind-base is ordinarily referred to as heartbase. The Mind-base is clearly stated in the Vibhanga, the second treatise of the Abhidhamma, to be non-material, vide the couplet section of Interrogation in Analysis of the Bases (para 171, section 2.)

A full course-of-cognition, also called a Thought-Process, occupies 17 thought-moments. Thoughts are either through one of the five sense-doors or through the mind-door.

When an object is presented to the mind through one of the five sense-doors, the course of cognition or thought-process runs as follows:

1. Past Bhavanga
2. Vibrating Bhavanga
3. Arrest Bhavanga
4. Sense-door Consciousness
5. Sense-Consciousness
6. Receiving Consciousness
7. Investigating Consciousness
8. Determining Consciousness
9. Impulson
10. Impulsion
11. Impulsion
12. Impulsion
13. Impulsion
14. Impulsion
15. Impulsion
16. Registering Consciousness
17. Registering Consciousness

When a sense object enters the field of presentation, it produces a perturbation in the stream of being at No. 2, and causes it to vibrate, which is arrested at No. 3 at the threshold of Consciousness.

At No. 4, the 5-door adverting arises, accomplishing the function of adverting, and it then ceases. The stimulus impinges on the 'sensitive' sense organ. It is here that a thought commences with the arising of attention which has to be present for a consciousness to arise.

There are 7 mind-constituents that must arise with every thought; they are a **sine qua non**, and attention is one of the 7 mind-constituents that arise.

It is a mind-element and not yet mind-consciousness. There are 3 mind-elements in all, namely,

a. sense-door consciousness which is attention
b. moral receiving consciousness and
c. immoral receiving consciousness

At No. 5, one of the 5 sense-consciousnesses arises, accomplishing the function of either seeing, or hearing, smelling, tasting, or touching, and then ceases.

At No. 6, the receiving consciousness arises accomplishing the consciousness of receiving. 3 more mind-constituents arise, namely, applied thought (**vitakka**), sustained thought (**vicara**) and belief or determination.

At No. 7, the investigating consciousness arises, accomplishing the function of investigating. Here begins mind-consciousness.

At No. 8, the determining consciousness arises, accomplishing the function of determining or deciding.

The impulsions at No. 9 to 15 called Javana are the moral or immoral consciousnesses which arise due to the, as it were, 'tasting' or enjoying the object.

The changing of an immoral to moral consciousness comes when the mind, after mental development, uses wisdom to change the moral direction of consciousness. This forms the pattern of all development, bringing into play mindfulness (**sati**), diligence (**viriya**) and wisdom (**panna**).

With Education and Mind-Culture, the Mind becomes associated with more and more experience and knowledge and wisdom. The Mind when you were young is not of the same calibre as when you are older.

It is at this Impulsion stage that karma is produced. Every volition has a karmic force which affects the germinal force.

The first of the karmical impulsive moments produces its karma-results during this life-time. If it cannot do so because the circumstances required for the taking place of the karma-result are missing or through preponderance of counter-active karma, it is karma that has lapsed (ahosi-karma). The 7th moment produces its karma-results in the next birth and if because the circumstances required for the taking place of the karma-result are missing or through the preponderance of counter-active karma, it is karma that has lapsed.

The 5 impulsions between the 1st and last ripen in some subsequent becoming and the karma-results never lapse, however long the round of rebirths.

After the 7 impulsions come the two registering consciousnesses, which are like the "after taste".

Sometimes an object is not strong enough to go to the Javana stage at No. 9. If you go along in a car, you have a fleeting glance at passers-by. The impressions are weak. But if you recognise a person, and you have some reactions about him or her, the impression is strong enough to go to No. 9 onwards.

For weak impressions, the thought does not begin at No. 4, and there will be more undercurrent subconsciousnesses to fill up the vacant places at the start, as it were; there may be 4 or 5 or 6 or more subconsciousnesses instead of the usual 3.

Acariya Buddhagosha has popularised the following simile to illustrate the process of cognition or perception on the occasion of a visible object. It is contained in U Pe Maung Tin's translation at p. 359 of Buddhagosha's Commentary, called the Atthasalini; this Commentary is on the first book of the Abhidhamma which is the Dhamma Sangani.

"A certain man with his head covered went to sleep at the foot of a fruiting mango tree. Then a ripe mango loosened from the stalk, fell to the ground, grazing his ear. Awakened by that sound, he opened his eyes and looked; then stretching out his hand he took the fruit, squeezed it, smelled it, and ate it. Herein, the time of his sleeping at the foot of the mango tree is as when we are subconsciously alive (bhavanga-sota);

the instant of the ripe mango falling from its stalk and grazing his ear is like the instant of the object striking the sentient organism (bhavanga-calana); the time of awaking through the sound is like that of adverting by the five sense-doors agitating the subconscious life continnum (panca-dvāra vajjana); the time of the man's opening his eyes and looking is like that of accomplishing the function of seeing through visual cognition (cakkhu-vinnana); the time of stretching out his hand and taking the mango is as that of the resultant mind-element receiving the object (Sanpaticchana); the time of taking it and squeezing it is as that of the resultant element of mind-cognition examining the object (santirana); the time of smelling it is as that of the inoperative element of mind-cognition determining the object (votthappana); the time of eating is as that of apperception (javana); enjoying the taste of the object (tadalambana)."

In this book we shall be referring off and on to the Law of Dependent Origination or Dependent Genesis. It can be referred to as and when required. It runs as follows:

1. **Avijjāpaccayā sankhāra:** "Through Ignorance are conditioned the sankhāran", i.e. the rebirth-producing volitions (cetanā) or "karma-formations" or "karma-accumulations". In other words, ignorance begets the karma-accumulations.

2. **Sankhāra-paccayā viññānam:** "Through the karma-formations (in past life) is conditioned Rebirth-Linking consciousness (in the present life).

3. **Viññāna-paccayā nāma-rūpam:** "Through Consciousness are conditioned the Mental and Physical Phenomena (nāma-rūpa) i.e. that which makes up our so called individual existence.

4. **Nāma-rūpa-paccayā salāyatanam:** "Through the Mental and Physical Phenomena are conditioned the 6 Bases", i.e. the 5 Physical sense organs, and consciousness as the sixth.

5. Salāyatana-paccayā phasso: "Through the six Bases is conditioned contact."
6. Phassa-paccayā vedanā: "Through contact is conditioned feeling".
7. Vedanā-paccayā tanhā: "Through Feeling is conditioned Craving".
8. Tanhā-paccayā upādānam: "Through craving is conditioned Clinging".
9. Upādāna-paccayā Bhavo: "Through Clinging is conditioned the process of Becoming", consisting in the active and the passive life-process, i.e., the rebirth producing karma-process (kamma-bhava) and, as its result, the Rebirth-process (upatti-bhava).
10. Bhava-paccayā jāti: "Through the (rebirth-producing karma) Process of Becoming is conditioned Rebirth".
11. Jāti-paccayā jarāmaranam: etc; "Through Rebirth are conditioned Old Age and
12. Death (sorrow, lamentation, pain, grief, and despair). Thus arises this whole mass of suffering again in the future".

The first 4 propositions in the Law of Dependent Origination say that

1. Ignorance begets karma-accumulations, and
2. Karma-accumulations in the past lives beget rebirth consciousness in the present life, and
3. Rebirth-Consciousness begets the mental and physical phenomena which make up our so-called individual existence, and
4. Mental and physical phenomena beget the six bases, namely, the 5 physical sense-organs, and Mind base as the sixth.

Ignorance means the forces of evil which are ever in this world, and can be summed up as not knowing the 4 Noble Truths as they really are, which was the subject of the

27

Buddha's First Sermon after attaining enlightenment under the Bodhi Tree. Like the forces of gravity, ignorance disposes us towards evil. It is only by some sort of education or mind development that one turns from darkness to light. This primordial evil has to be dissipated so that we turn towards wisdom. So, either by concentration or meditation, the two forms of mental development, we come towards the realisation of good. It is only by repeated concentration and meditation, using mindfulness and diligence and wisdom, that we gradually arrive at better, and more moral, dispositions.

This ignorance in the past existences produces the karma-accumulations that will determine your rebirth in this existence. Your genes and your chromosomes and your DNA and RNA are determined by your past karma. At the time of conception your past karma has fashioned your body or tactile sense, and your heart base on which your future Mind will depend, and your masculinity or femininity. Later will come your 'sensitive' eye, your 'sensitive' ear, your 'sensitive' nose and your 'sensitive' tongue.

We use the word 'sensitive' eye, because it is not the whole organ of the eye that is intended, but only that extremely subtle point at which it may be said that the purely physical activity of visual structure ends and consciousness of that stimulation begins.

It is that locus which forms a common frontier between the impact of an appropriate sense stimulus and the arising of a conscious state as the result of that stimulus.

The word 'sensitive' is thus used to denote that part of each of your five senses, which will be the basis of your sense-consciousnesses, namely, the visual consciousness, the auditory consciousness and so on, including the mind-consciousness dependent on the mind-door. It is as the result of the sense-organs that we come to realise the external world, and we are becoming aware of what our sense stimuli or sense impressions are conveying to our brain.

As the result of our rebirth linking consciousness come the mental and physical phenomena which make up your so-called individual existence.

Then come the 6 bases. It is only some time after birth that the 6 bases are fully developed. From another point of view, there are 6 sense-organs, termed internal bases, which possess the property of enabling that Consciousness to arise into activity when they are impinged upon by an appropriate stimulus. They are the sense bases.

Then, there are the sense-objects, called external bases, which give to objects their innate properties of bringing the senses into activity when under appropriate conditions they impinge upon them. They are called the object bases, namely visible (visual) base, ear base, etc.

The 6-sense bases consist of material qualities derived from the 4 Great Primaries or Essentials. These material qualities are of an extremely subtle and special nature, for it is by way of these internal bases and their contact with the external stimulus of object, that active consciousness concerning the object is able to arise.

It is a wondrous 6-sense Organism which produces Consciousnesses of different kinds when a material thing or idea, called the object, comes in contact with a sense-organ, which is another material thing.

The 5th proposition of the Law of Dependent Origination says that the six bases beget contact. Contact is the conjunction of the inner and outer bases to produce feeling of the 6th proposition.

The 7th proposition is that feeling begets craving. This craving is one of the most important words in Buddhism, for we will come to learn in the Second Noble Truth that craving is the cause of suffering. Once we understand what Craving is, in its myriads of forms, and that it is subjective, we have mastered the basis of life.

The 8th proposition brings us to Grasping or Clinging, which is a bigger edition of Craving. It is the intermittent striving after craving because we like it. The 5-clinging Aggregates, much deprecated by the Buddha, are explained in the next Chapter.

In the 9th proposition comes Becoming. Becoming means achievement. You study hard when you are young in order to achieve something. Here it is an ultimate and it refers to that terrific urge to be reborn. 'Becoming' brings about rebirth in the future.

In the 10th proposition, becoming begets Birth. It means the birth of anything, from the highest to the lowest. We have momentary Birth all the time. When Consciousness arises and disappears immediately, other consciousnesses arise; this is Birth.

Birth is inexorably followed by old age and death, with its accompaniments of sorrow, lamentation, pain, grief and despair.

The aim of Buddhism is to bring about the cessation of the sequence of Dependent origination. It is mostly done by the elimination of craving through the 8-fold Noble or Constituent Path, which is the 4th Noble Truth.

Consciousnesses have been classified and classified, and again classified. There are in all 89 possible consciousnesses, namely 81 mundane and 8 supramundane.

The detailed classification is types. An example of a type of moral consciousness is "unprompted, accompanied by pleasure, combined with knowledge".

An example of a type of immoral consciousness is "prompted, accompanied by pleasure, and unaccompanied by knowledge".

But these classifications should not bother us.

If the eight supramundane consciousnesses are expanded, we get forty supramundane consciousnesses making the whole range 121 consciousnesses, namely 81 + 40.

There are 4 main divisions of consciousness, the first 3 pertaining to the 3 mundane realms or spheres of existence, and the fourth is the supramundane.

From the moral point of view, there are 3 kinds of consciousnesses, namely, good, bad or neutral. Whether a consciousness is good or bad depends on its roots. They are mind-constituents.

Consciousness

The bad roots are:
1. Greed
2. Anger or hatred
3. Delusion

The good roots are the opposites of the bad ones, namely,
1. Goodwill
2. Love
3. Wisdom

The neutrals are with or without roots.

The breakdown of these 89 consciousnesses is as follows:
1. Sensuous Realm ... 54 consciousnesses
2. Pure Form ... 15 consciousnesses
3. Non-Form ... 12 consciousnesses

Total: 81

4. Supra-Mundane ... 8 consciousnesses

Grand Total: 89

The Stream Entrant Stage has its Path Consciousness and Fruition Consciousness, the Once-Returner Stage has its Path and Fruition consciousnesses, the Non-Returner Stage has its Path and Fruition consciousnesses, and the Holy One Stage has its Path and Fruition consciousnesses, making in all 8 Supra-Mundane Consciousnesses.

31

Chapter 3

The 5-Aggregates

The human Personality consists of 5 Aggregates namely,
1. Matter Aggregate
2. Consciousness Aggregate
3. Feeling Aggregate
4. Perception and Memory Aggregate
5. Mental Formations Aggregate, composed of the remaining 50 mental constituents or factors.

They are the basic components of a being.

The usual formula for an Aggregate is: "Past, present or future, one's own or external, gross or subtle, lofty or low, far or near."

These are 11 different distinctions that go to make up an Aggregate. It will be seen that every conceivable kind is included. All this will be explained later when we are doing Insight Meditation.

The same formula pertains to each of the 5 Aggregates.

Understanding of the 5-Aggregates plays a big part in Buddhism. These 5-Aggregates, viewed in another way, can be divided into Mind and Matter, or rather, Mentality and Materiality.

Whenever Consciousness arises, there arise also the Feeling Aggregate and the Perception Aggregate and the Mental Formations Aggregate. These are the four Mental Aggregates. The Matter Aggregate is generated simultaneously by the four generators, viz, karma, consciousness, temperature and nutriment. This makes up the 5 Aggregates.

These 5 Aggregates come from nowhere and go to nowhere. They just arise and disappear. This concept is very important in Buddhist Meditation. The 5 Aggregates are evanescent. They just flash forth and disappear.

One Mind succeeds another: the 5-Aggregates arise and disappear immediately. Consciousness can arise through any of the 6 Doors. The 5-Aggregates that arise from the Eye-Door are different in kind to the 5-Aggregates that arise through the Ear-Door, and again are different in kind to the Aggregates that arise through the Nose-Door, etc.

The conjunction of the 4 conditions, namely, 1. The Mind Door, 2. an ideational object, 3. undercurrent subconsciousness and 4. attention, produces Mind-Consciousness. It means that this Mind-Consciousness is a result. Simultaneously there arise the 3 other mental Aggregates, namely, Feeling Aggregate, Perception Aggregate and the Mental-Formations Aggregate. These 4 Aggregates constitute Mentality.

Along with the 4 Aggregates of Mentality arise the thought-produced materiality, among others, and the result is the 5-Aggregates.

It is all automatic. It will be seen that the 'I' or self does not enter into the picture at all. However, the Mind-Consciousness, which is the Big Magician, brings in the ideas of 'I' and Mine and Myself, and therefore there is attachment to these 5-Aggregates.

The Buddha said that the 5-Aggregates are harmless and even Arahats have the 5-Aggregates. But it is the attachment to them that is deprecated: we will see later that this attachment constitutes suffering.

We have seen how these 5-Aggregates arise and how they disappear immediately — arising and cessation, and once again arising and cessation, and so on. They just flash forth when the conditions are fulfilled and immediately disappear; they are evanescent.

To explain the arising of the 5-Aggregates, it will be best to quote from the Rev. Nyanatiloka's Buddhist Dictionary.

I have put in bold print the words **evanescent** and **flashing forth**.

"KHANDHA: The 5 'Groups', or 'Groups of clinging (upādāna-kkhandha) are the 5 aspects in which the Buddha has summed up all the physical and mental phenomena of existence, and which appear to the ignorant man as his Ego, or personality, to wit:

1. the Corporeality group (rūpa-kkhandha)
2. the Feeling (vedanā-kkhandha)
3. the Perception (sannā-kkhandha)
4. the Mental-Formation (sankhāra-kkhandha)
5. the Consciousness (viññana-kkhandha)."

Whatever there exists of corporeal things, whether past, present or future, one's own or external, gross or subtle, lofty or low, far or near, all that belongs to the Corporeality-group. Whatever there exists of feeling . . . of perception . . . of mental formations . . . of consciousness . . . all that belongs to the Consciousness-group".

"This so-called individual existence is in reality nothing but a mere process of those mental and physical phenomena, a process that since time immemorial has been going on, and that also after the so-called death will still continue for unthinkably long periods of times. These 5 groups, however, neither singly nor collectively constitute any self-dependent real Ego-entity, or Personality (atta), nor is there to be found any such entity apart from them. Hence the belief in such an Ego-entity or

Personality, as real in the ultimate sense, proves a mere illusion.

> "When all constituent parts are there,
> The designation 'cart' is used;
> Just so, where the 5 groups exist,
> of 'living being' do we speak"

"The fact ought to be emphasised here that the 5 groups, correctly speaking merely form an abstract classification by the Buddha, but that they as such, i.e. as just these 5 complete groups, have no real existence, since, apart from corporeality and a number of mental formations, only single representatives of these groups can arise with any state of consciousness. For example, with one and the same unit of consciousness only one single kind of feeling, say joy or sorrow, can be associated, and never more than one. Similarly two different perceptions cannot arise at the same moment. Also, of the various kinds of sense cognition or consciousness, only one single one can be present at a time, for example, seeing, hearing or inner consciousness, etc. Of the 50 mental formations, however, a smaller or larger number are always associated with every state of consciousness, as we shall see later on.

"Due to lack of understanding is also the fact that the 5 **Khandhas** are often conceived as too compact, too substantial, so to speak, as more or less permanent entities, whereas in reality, as already stated, they as such, never exist; and even their representatives have only an **evanescent** existence. Feeling, perception and mental formations, e.g., form merely the various aspects of those single units of consciousness which, like lightning, **flash forth** at every moment and immediately thereafter disappear again. They are to consciousness what redness, softness, sweetness, etc., are to the apple, and have no more reality than these things.

"In S.XXII. 56 there is given a short definition of these 5 groups, namely: What, O Monks, is the Corporeality-Group? The 4 primary elements (**mahā-bhūta** or **dhātu**) and corporeality depending thereon, this is called the corporeality-group.

"What, O Monks, is the Feeling-Group? There are 5 classes of feeling: due to visual impression, to sound impression, to odour impression, to taste impression, to bodily impression and to mind impression . . .

"What, O Monks, is the Perception-Group? There are 6 classes of perception: perception of visual objects, of sounds, of odours, of tastes, of bodily impression and of mental impressions . . .

"What, O Monks, is the Group of Mental Formations? There are 6 classes of volitional states (cetana): with regard to visual objects, to sounds, to odours, to tastes, to bodily impressions, and to mind objects . . .

"What, O Monks, is the Consciousness-Group? There are 6 classes of consciousness, nose-consciousness, tongue-consciousness, eye-consciousness, ear-consciousness, body-consciousness, and mind-consciousness."

The 5-Aggregates are also known as 5-Resultant Aggregates as they are the result of past existences. As the functions like bathing, dressing, eating, etc., are performed, no results are produced for the future existences. One may experience bodily suffering, but in the case of an Arahat, he has no mental suffering, like worry, anxiety, grief, etc., which cause future existences.

It is unwise reflection or recollection on the 5-Aggregates that bring forth the 5-Clinging or Grasping Aggregates.

The 5-Aggregates are subjective whereas the 5-Clinging Aggregates are objective, being 'objects of Clinging'. This will be clearer as we proceed.

The 5-Resultant Aggregates arise from Consciousness, Mentality-Materiality, 6 Bases, Contact and Feeling. The 5-Clinging Aggregates arise when there are Ignorance, Formations, Craving, Clinging and Becoming. They cause the 5-Clinging Aggregates, as and when they are made to arise, by unwise thinking, attention, reflection, planning, recollections.

It is due to clinging that the 5-Clinging Aggregates and the corruptions arise. For example, the Mind takes the subjective person as the object of reflection, and remarks are made such as, 'What a clever man I am', 'I am handsome', there is clinging to the person (materiality & mentality) as 'I' at those times. It is something more than the normal or ordinary workings of the mind. It is extra workings of the Mind. The clinging is accompanied by the corruption of conceit.

When the Mind takes the son, for example, as the object of reflection and there is anxiety as to whether he will pass the examination or make good in life, there is clinging to the son as 'mine' and the corruption of anxiety or worry arises.

These mental actions of reflection, recollection, etc., result in likes, dislikes, fear, worry, anxiety and other corruptions. The mind is disquieted, distressed, disturbed, and we will learn later that this is suffering.

In the Sutta-Nikayas, called kindred sayings, dealing with Aggregate, in one of the Discourses, it is said that the 5-Aggregates become clinging Aggregates when there are Intoxicants, Cankers, Biases.

There are 4 kinds of Intoxicants:

1. Intoxicant of Sensuality
2. Intoxicant of Renewed Existence
3. Intoxicant of Speculative Opinion
4. Intoxicant of Ignorance

1. The Intoxicant of Sensuality, that sensual desire, sensual passion, sensual delight, sensual craving, sensual fondness, sensual thirst, sensual fever, sensual rapacity, which is the result of the pleasures of the senses.

2. The Intoxicant of Renewed Existence, the desire, the passion for coming into being, delight in coming into being, craving, fondness for coming into being, the fever, the yearning, the hungering to come into being, which is felt concerning rebirths.

3. The Intoxicant of speculative opinion, or wrong views. You don't know you have a wrong view. You have a craving for your view. You think that whatever you do is right. You think, 'I' know'. The craving here is based on love of yourself.

4. The Intoxicant of ignorance, of ignorance of the 4-Noble Truths. You do not know Correctly. You have built a monastery and you are looked up to and you love it; it is a form of craving. Ignorance exists always along with craving. Ignorance is the cause and craving is the effect.

So there is always a streak of Craving in all the differing forms of Intoxicants.

Craving, Conceit and Wrong View. It is the last which is eradicated first.

It means that there are 3 Forms or Aspects of Self in Buddhism.

1. Possessive or Craving Self
2. Conceit Self
3. Wrong View Self

All the time, the worldling is running after different objects of sense and the mind-sense. There is seeing, and hearing, and tasting, etc. There arises the idea of 'I see', 'I hear', 'I taste', etc. There is really no 'I', but the Mind-Consciousness has bluffed the worldling by injecting the idea of "I".

As Wrong View has to be eradicated first, before one becomes a Stream Entrant, let us deal with it first. It is Wrong View or Wrong Belief.

When you meet a person, how do you recognise him, or distinguish him from others? By his exterior form, by his exterior body. Others recognise you similarly.

We know that only ultimates are realities and all the rest are conventional concepts and terms. If this form or body is taken as 'I' or Self, it is wrong view regarding what is not an ultimate reality.

There is wrong view regarding an ultimate constituent of oneself. We cannot see an ultimate with the naked eye, but know it with the inner eye. Take, for instance, the ultimates behind the 5-Aggregates which are composites and therefore conventional terms. These ultimates may be rightly viewed by you as mere ultimates, but if you wrongly view these ultimates as self, it is **sakkaya-ditthi**.

The human body exists. This statement is on a par with the statement that water exists. It is a conventional term.

Water is not an ultimate reality and the human body is not an ultimate reality. The human body is composed of atoms and cells.

The Buddha was at pains to point out that the human body is not an ultimate and that there are 32 constituent parts of the body, so that the worldling will know that a human body was a composite, just as a 'chariot' was a composite.

And again, none of the 32 constituent parts is ultimate.

The human being is not 'I' or mine. It is a perversion of thinking that the human body is 'I' or mine or Myself.

The 'I' is a mental concept. There is no physical basis for the concept of 'I'.

We know that the mental part consists of the 4 Mental Aggregates, namely Consciousness, Feelings, Perception and Formations. Where is the 'I'? It is the work of Mind-consciousness, the Big Magician, to inject the idea of an 'I'. It is just a perversion. The Buddha asks us not to be bluffed by the Big Magician.

Life consists of natural processes that function by themselves and we should not put a self into it.

We have been stressing the fact that it is not the 'I', but that it is the Mind that motivates everything.

The Buddha's Teaching is the Middle Way. It says that Eternity Belief and Annihilation Belief are wrong.

Eternity Belief is the existence of a persisting Ego-Entity or Individuality existing independently of physical and mental processes that constitutes life, and continuing even after death.

Annihilation Belief is the belief in the existence of an Ego-Entity or personality which is annihilated at death.

The Buddha, however, teaches that the Personality or Ego are but conventional designations, whilst in the ultimate sense there is only this process of physical and mental phenomena which continually arise and disappear immediately.

The Buddha has dissected the Body and Mind into its constituent parts, namely the 5-Aggregates, i.e., the Matter Aggregate, and the Mind having four Aggregates, namely, Consciousness, Feelings, Perception and Mental Formations and nothing more. There is no soul whatever.

The Conceit self is eradicated only when one becomes an Arahat. Conceit is of many kinds and forms and some are enumerated thus: conceit of accomplishment, of appearance, of bearing, of birth, of bodily perfection, of bodily proportion, being not despised, of dexterity, erudition, gain, having adherents, health, being honoured, intelligence, of kinsmen, being an acknowledged authority, being moral, of prominence, popularity, being respected, tall, wealth, youth, etc. Also the ideas 'I am better' 'I am equal'.

The Possessive or Craving Self is similarly eradicated only on becoming an Arahat.

Craving is the cause of suffering, as will be explained in the exposition of the 4-Noble Truths, and craving is the cause of continuing the cycle of rebirths.

Craving is of 3 kinds: 1. craving for sense pleasures, 2. craving for existence, and   3. craving for self-annihilation.

Craving is of many forms, and is very cunning. There is craving when there does not seem to be any that is apparent. It is quite a job to ferret out this craving.

Practically the most important Teaching of the Buddha is that there is no Self. If you believe in a Self, you will act in one way, but if you believe there is no Self, you will act in another way.

It is with Wisdom that you come to know that there is no Self. The teaching of Craving, Conceit and Wrong View, the Teaching of the 4-Noble Truths of Suffering, the Teaching of Impermanence, Suffering and No Self, in fact the whole of the Abhidhamma is calculated to make you know that there is no Self, that there is no soul, namely, everything is No-Self.

Say, you own a piece of land. If you think that you will find petroleum or gems in your land, you will dig. If you have not found it yet, on your death-bed you will ask your children to go on digging.

But if you are sure in your life-time that there is no petroleum or gems in your land, you will not follow the useless task of digging your land.

Similarly, if you are sure that there is no soul or self within your body, you will eschew certain acts which you are sure is a waste of time.

Chapter 4

Mind and Matter

Let us learn something more about Mind and Matter. The function of the Mind to see is dependent on the sensitive eye. If the sensitive eye does not function or is absent, as in the case of the blind, no mind arises to see.

The function of the Mind to hear is dependent on the sensitive ear. Similarly for the other sense-objects, and the function of the Mind to see, hear, smell, etc., is dependent on their corresponding senses.

There are different types of Mind. The Mind that sees is not the same as that which hears. When you see someone, the Mind arises where the object is visual form; then you hear a sound, and the Mind arises with the sound as its object. But the visual Mind has to cease before the auditory Mind can commence. So a new Mind arises with every new object.

Take a visual consciousness. The Mind-consciousness follows to recall the immediately past visual object, and, based on it, takes colour, shapes, persons, and things, and also thinks about them.

Take as ear-consciousness (of sound waves within the ear's physical range). The Mind-consciousness follows to recall the immediately past sound, and distinguish it from sounds previously heard so as to know whether it is that of a gun or a bell.

Supposing that it is the sound of a gun. We have ear-consciousness at first. Other consciousnesses follow to recall the sound, and investigate and determine what it is. When it is determined that it is the sound of a gun, a mental reaction of fright will occur, but not in the case of a child or those who do not know what a gun can do. It means that whether you are disturbed or not depends on your mental responses.

In the act of hearing, the mental processes are:

1. the mind hears a sound (ear consciousness).
2. a new mind recalls the word it has associated with the sound e.g. dog.
3. a new mind projects the word, dog, on to the sound and takes it as an object of the Mind.
4. a new mind mentally reads the word (dog).

The word 'dog' is superimposed on the sound. Actually, the word and the sound are taken as one, which of course is wrong.

Take the sounds from a radio. If a Chinese song or talk emanates from the loud-speaker, you cannot understand a word of it; the words are not mentally connected up to give sense to the sounds.

You must remember that only sounds are emitted from a radio, but you normally think that you hear words from the radio. Why? Because when the word associated with the sound appears, it has come from the mind. The word originated in the mind and therefore exists only in the mind. When we were young and learning to speak, particular words were associated with certain sounds. It means that sounds and words are two different things, but we are wrongly apt to think them as one. We have actually superimposed the word on the sound. And these words are connected up to get the ideas behind them.

Take the case of a person looking at an aeroplane in the sky. A second person comes along and he also looks up at the aeroplane in the sky. Actually, the second person could look at the first person or look at the plane, but in actual fact he looks at the plane, as if the first person was directing him to do so. Similarly for a third person or a fourth person; they all look up at the aeroplane in the sky.

Instead of a person, let us think in terms of Mind. The first Mind is aware of the aeroplane, and we know that the Mind disappears immediately.

A second Mind comes along. As if the first Mind has directed the second Mind to do so, it will be aware of the plane. Actually the second Mind could turn its attention to the aeroplane or be aware of the first Mind. But can it be aware of the first Mind? It cannot be aware straight away but must recall the first Mind after it has disappeared. It means that if the second Mind were to turn to the subject which is the first Mind, it becomes the object and ceases to be the subject.

Even then, if we recall the past Mind, we are on the way to mind the Mind.

But it will never do just to keep minding the Mind, for in order to learn anything, in the classroom or elsewhere, the Mind must be minding the objects and thinking about them and motivating verbal and physical actions. That is how meanings are given to the sequence of events, conclusions arrived at and practical results obtained.

Take, for instance, the act of seeing a car. The mental processes are:

1. The Mind knows the car as an external object.
2. A second Mind calls up in the Mind the name which is 'Car', and this name is the object of the Mind.
3. A new Mind mentally projects the name on to the thing; the mentally projected name is an object within the mind.
4. A new Mind takes the mentally projected name as an object within the Mind.

The above is expressed in the simplest and barest of terms. However, for a person to say, 'I see a rose', there arise complicated processes of imagination, reproductive and constructive, memory, conception, discrimination, judgement, classification, which all follow one another so rapidly in succession that the percipient considers that he 'sees' the rose almost instantaeously.

The reader who is interested in the mental processes involved can look it up on p. 32 of U Shwe Zan Aung's Introductory Essay to the Compendium of Philosophy which is the translation of Abhidhammatha-Sangaha, a sort of Vade-Mecum written by Anuruddha Thera of Ceylon in about the 8th Century. The translation is rather difficult reading, and was first published in 1910.

It must here be noted that the name is always an object within the mind and is not independent of the mind. But the thing and the name are taken to be one and the same; this is a perversion.

When we want to communicate about anything to others, we must use names, for the name calls up the thing to the minds of those who have also associated the name with the thing. That is how we employ nouns to distinguish one thing from another. A noun is the name given to the thing.

The thing is called a car; here the car is the name or noun. The thing and the name are two different things.

But we usually say, 'This is a car', 'to buy a car', as if the name and the thing are one and the same. We should really say, 'this is called a car'.

That is how wrong views about names and nouns come to be held.

We must remember that names are mind-made words. We must understand that the names exist only as objects of the mind, and not as objects outside or independent of the Mind.

A car is not a single thing but made up of different parts which are inter-dependent. 'Car' is a conventional word.

Similarly, take the case of the name 'John'. Instead of knowing that the name 'John' is only a name, it is believed that John is an external object independent of the Mind. But it is thought that John and one's person are one and the same.

Take the case of mental labelling of one's person as 'I'. Instead of one's name, one usually uses the pronoun 'I' to designate one's person in speech and writing. 'I', like the name 'John' is only a mental label which exists momentarily in the Mind. 'I' exists only when mentally and verbally said. But we say 'I see', 'I hear', etc., all the time. 'I' is regarded as the subject, when it is only a mental label. The good thing about mind-consciousness is that it synthesises and connects up different minds. Take for example a lump, or a grain, of sugar. The first Mind sees the thing — visual consciousness. The second Mind grasps the name of the thing as sugar. The third Mind tastes the thing called sugar — gustatory consciousness — and finds it sweet. The fourth Mind pronounces that sugar is sweet.

Without the connecting up, we could not understand the happenings and experiences of the world.

Let us now turn to a consideration of Matter. The 4 Primary Essential Qualities or Properties of Matter are:

1. manifestation as Hardness
2. manifestation as Cohesion
3. manifestation as Heat
4. \manifestation as Resistance to Motion.

These 4 properties are separate but exist together. They function jointly, yet severally.

You can visualise their opposite qualities only by comparison. You see the colours of black and white only by comparison. You know good health only when you come to know bad health.

Changeability is the very essence of matter. Matter is changing all the time, and matter and changeability are synonymous.

Hardness. This is hardness, and by comparison, softness. For instance, soft food gradually hardens. When you cook meat and apply heat, it gradually softens. You know the quality of hardness with the inner eye. Hardness is the very basis of the other 3 Primaries.

Cohesion. Cohesion is the quality of cohesion and inherence and growth. If there is no cohesion, matter would disintegrate. In a building, cement, expressed in conventional terms, binds, but with your inner eye or brain, you know cohesion namely the quality of coherence. In oceans and mountains and everything it is cohesion. A lump of gold coheres. A road surface coheres. Your human body and parts of it cohere. Trees grow due to the quality of cohesion. If you add water to flour, it becomes pliable due to cohesion.

Heat. Heat or lack of heat. The human body has heat. The heat is changing all the time. The essence of matter is change, which must be seen by the inner eye. Take wax; when you apply heat, it softens. You can visualise the **heat** and **cohesion** with the inner eye. All these qualities are ultimates.

Motion. Motion and resistance to motion. If you pump air into a tyre, it gets hard and there is resistance to motion. If you deflate the tyre, there is less resistance to motion. You know **Motion** with the inner eye. Inside the human body, there is always pushing and pulling. In-breathing and out-breathing are manifestations of Motion.

These 4 Primaries always act together and thus there is strength. If you take away one, all come to naught.

This manifestation is in everything. They are the same, wherever they are manifested.

Electricity and Magnetism are different conventionally, but as ultimates, the manifestation is the same.

Buddha taught that the human body is composed of cells, called **kalāpas**. We know about the octad consisting of Hardness, Cohesion, Heat and Motion, and the 4 secondary qualities of colour, smell, taste and nutriment.

Add psychic life and we get the nonad. Add each of the sensitive parts of the sense-organs, and we get the decads. Thus octad + Psychic life = nonad.

The decad cells are:
- nonad + visual sensitive part,
- nonad + hearing sensitive part,
- nonad + smell sensitive part,
- nonad + taste sensitive part,
- nonad + body sensitive part,
- nonad + heart sensitive part.

However, the Abhidhamma denies the existence of the heart-base as physical.

We have cells not only consisting of 10 qualities, but also of 11 qualities, 12 qualities and 13 qualities, but they are not of immediate value to us.

All these cells have space in between. There is nothing that has not space in between.

Impermanence, Suffering and No-Self

These 3 concepts are basic to Buddhism. They are the marks or characteristics of existence. In Pali, it is said:

> sabbe sankhāra anicca
> sabbe sankhāra dukkha
> sabbe dhamma anatta

Sankhāra here means anything conditioned; conditioned means created or made to arise.

So everything created or made to arise is impermanent.

We have seen how consciousness arises. When the conditions have been fulfilled, nothing will prevent consciousness from arising.

In the Pali utterance that all dhammas are non-self, 'dhamma' means everything in the world, and is more comprehensive than the word sankhāra. It states that everything in the world is no-self.

The word 'states', to mean dhamma, is used in a very broad sense, for it refers not only to states of consciousness but also the mental constituents, and also the 4 Great Primaries or Essentials and their dependent material qualities and even Nirvana.

Impermanence

When we know that the 5-Aggregates arise and then immediately disappear, it is not difficult to visualise that such things are impermanent. They are born and then die.

Not only in modern science but also in Buddhism there are cells. In the human body there are millions of atoms and cells. They consist of the 4-Primaries and are called cells; these cells arise and disappear. The old is succeeded by the new, giving rise to the concept of Impermanence.

If you stop the fuel generating these 4 Primaries, they die. If one of them dies, all die together. If Body ceases, then Mentality ceases, for Mentality is dependent on Materiality for its arising.

Suffering

The 4 Noble Truths of Suffering were discovered by the Buddha. They form the very core of his Teaching and have been incorporated in the next Chapter. **Impermanence, Suffering and No-Self** are interdependent concepts. If you understand one thoroughly, you understand all three.

No-Self

All philosophies devised by man are meant to explain the reason for his existence. There is a great desire to continue to exist after death and he has succeeded in inventing many different philosophical and religious systems. He wants to be satisfied that there will be a next world to go to, and speaks of revelations and produces arguments to support his views. It is his craving for further existence that makes him believe strongly in the ideas that he has invented himself. In order that there may be something to continue on, he says that there is a soul or spirit which is eternal.

However, Buddha came to realise when he was enlightened under the Bodhi Tree that the idea of a soul was unnecessary. He saw that the 5-Aggregates, which are changing all the time, arose and passed away according to fixed laws of Dependent Origination. There was no need for a soul.

It was soon after his Enlightenment that he intuitively acquired the System of Analysis which we now know as Abhidhamma. His analytical Method enabled beings gradually to be able to see things as they really are, and to destroy the conditioned state, and thereby attain Nirvana.

Buddhism is the only religion that promises its summum bonum during this existence.

The concept of a soul is unnecessary to an understanding of the structural nature of beings. Everything is classified under one or other of the 5-Aggregates. No quality or feature that is in any way discernible falls outside this five-fold system of classification.

It is activity in the form of volition based on craving which bound these aggregates together.

These aggregates arose, and passed away, in accordance with the fixed laws of Dependent Origination. The idea of a soul was quite unnecessary and the real 'creator' was craving based on ignorance. The whole process of existence, past, present and future, occurred strictly in accordance with laws, without the need for a soul or even a God.

Beings, regardless of the plane in which they are born, do not possess any permanent identity, personality, self, soul or spirit, but are temporary manifestations of several constituents or aggregates which themselves, though changing, nevertheless show continuity of process. Thus the expression 'rebirth' is not to be understood that the same being in one existence is reborn into a future existence by virtue of there being a soul or spirit as a factor providing inherent continuity.

The new being has no direct relationship to its predecessor, by way of a permanent unchanging soul or spirit, but is nevertheless the direct outcome or resultant of the activities of that predecessor. There is a current of constant change and no stability of any kind.

The **Anatta** Doctrine must be understood in 3 different ways:

1. There is no soul.
2. There is no Self.
3. There is no Control.

The human body does not exist in terms of ultimates; this is on a par with the statement that water exists in terms of conventional truth, but does not exist in terms of ultimate truth, in reality.

The human Personality or Ego-entity is composed of 5-Aggregates subjectively and 5-Clinging Aggregates objectively. There is nothing more than that in the human make-up. The Buddha has shown that none of the Aggregates is a Self, and that therefore there is no Self.

Neither within these bodily and mental phenomena of existence, nor outside of them, can be found anything that in the ultimate sense could be regarded as a self-reliant real Ego-entity, personality or any other abiding substance. The Buddha taught the impersonality of all existence, and that there exists only this continual process of arising and passing bodily and mental phenomena, and that there is no separate Ego-entity within or without the process.

As for the third idea that there is no real Control over bodily processes, the human body carries out its bodily functions automatically. It is like a chemist watching the functions of a chemical reaction; once the conditions are there, the reaction is performed automatically. Similarly, the human body performs automatically.

Inexorably there is growth. Inexorably there is decay, old age and death. It is anatta.

Chapter 5

The 4 Noble Truths

1ST NOBLE TRUTH

Suffering is an experience that is common to all sentient beings. There exists no experience which is equally universal. It is the fundamental thesis of a world-embracing thought.

All sentient beings endure suffering because all are subject to old age, decay and death. It unites the human and the animal kingdoms and is the foundation of a universal brotherhood.

The opening verse of the tenth chapter of the Dhammapada runs as follows: "All beings are afraid of dying, all beings are afraid of death".

Without fully understanding this axiomatic truth of suffering and the cause of suffering, one cannot really understand the other parts of his teaching. And Buddhism becomes easy when the Second Noble Truth regarding the cause of Suffering is really understood.

It was this experience of common suffering and the resolve to conquer the problem of birth and death that caused Prince Siddartha to renounce his kingdom.

Under the Bodhi Tree, he came to understand what the Mind was and its illusory nature. He conquered the delusions and perversions caused by the Mind, and, meditating on the ultimates, he achieved Enlightenment at the dawn of the next day.

The 4 Noble Truths

After ruminating on his achievements for a few weeks, he thought that he would contact his former 5 companions. So he walked from Buddha-Gaya to Sarnath near Benares. When he reached his 5 colleagues, they would have nothing to do with him, as one who had gone back to normal life.

He told them that he had reached Enlightenment, that he had become the Buddha. They refused to believe him, but he eventually prevailed upon them to listen to him.

He expounded to them the Law of Suffering, which had been expounded by all the Buddhas.

It was the usual formula. Take the case of hatred; it is:
1. the arising of hatred;
2. the cause of the arising of hatred;
3. the cessation of hatred;
4. the Path leading to the cessation of hatred.

In this case, it was the Law of Dukkha or Suffering, usually termed the 4 Noble Truths of Suffering, viz.,
1. The Noble Truth of Suffering
2. The Noble Truth of the Origin of Suffering
3. The Noble Truth of the Cessation of Suffering
4. The Noble Truth of the Path leading to the cessation of suffering which are the 8 Constituents or Factors of the Noble Eightfold Path.

The Pali word is 'Dukkha'. It is a very wide term and western authors have translated it usually as suffering; suffering is too strong a word for it. It means unsatisfactoriness, disappointment, ill, and many other synonyms.

The 5 companions were used to concepts in conventional language. Herewith, in the Digha-Nikaya, (Sutta 22) is the description of Suffering in conventional terms.

"What, now, is the Noble Truth of Suffering? Birth is suffering; Decay is suffering; Death is suffering; Sorrow, Lamentation, Pain, Grief, and Despair are suffering; not to get what one desires is Suffering; in short, the 5 Groups of existence are suffering.

"What now is Birth? The Birth of beings belonging to this or that order of beings, their being born, their conception and springing into existence, the manifestation of the Groups of Existence, the springing of sense-activity — this is called Birth.

"And what is Decay? The Decay of beings belonging to this or that order of beings, their getting aged, frail, grey, and wrinkled, the falling of their vital force, the wearing out of the senses — this is called decay.

"And what is Death? The departing and vanishing of beings out of this or that order of beings, their destruction, disappearance, death, the completion of their life-period, dissolution of the Groups of Existence, the discarding of the body — this is called death.

"And what is sorrow? The sorrow arising through this or that loss or misfortune which one encounters, the worrying oneself, the state of being alarmed, inward sorrow, inward woe — this is called sorrow.

"And what is Lamentation? Whatsoever, through this or that loss or misfortune which befalls one, is wail and lament, wailing and lamenting the state of woe and lamentation — this is called lamentation.

"And what is Pain? The bodily pain and unpleasantness, the painful and unpleasant feeling produced by bodily impression — this is called Pain.

"And what is Grief? The mental pain and unpleasantness, the painful and unpleasant feeling produced by mental impression — this is called Grief.

"And what is Despair? Distress and despair arising through this or that loss or misfortune which one encounters, distressfulness, and desperation — this is called despair.

"And what is the 'suffering of not getting what one desires'? To beings subject to birth there come the desires; 'O that we were not subject to birth! O, that no new birth was before us: Subject to decay, disease, death, sorrow, lamentation, pain, grief and despair, the desire comes to them: O, that we were not subject to these things: O, that these things were not before us'. But this cannot be got by mere desiring; and not to get what one desires, is suffering."

Also, being associated with those you do not like is suffering, and not being associated with those whom you want to be associated with is suffering.

However, the Buddha now talked to them in a different fashion for they now heard him talk of ultimates, namely, of ultimate realities in Body and ultimates in Mind. He explained to them how the 5-Aggregates arose. But when the idea of 'I' and mine and my body is injected into the 5-Aggregates, they become the 5-Clinging Aggregates. It is attachment to these 5-Aggregates that is suffering.

The very first night the leader became a 'stream-entrant'.

He carried on the discourse for four more nights, talking of ultimates, and it is said that at the end of each night, a new companion became a Stream-Entrant, so that they had all become Stream-Entrants by the end of the fifth night.

After that, he discoursed in detail on the Doctrine of **Anatta**. Of course, they all had realised that **Anatta** meant no soul, no substance and no control over life processes. What he had previously thought were souls that transmigrated from existence to existence were discovered by him under the Bodhi Tree to be karmic-energies that were transmitted from existence to existence.

By the end of the Discourse, the 5 Vaggi had all become Arahats.

2ND NOBLE TRUTH

The Second Noble Truth of the Origin of Suffering says that Craving is the cause of Suffering. Craving is variously known as craving, sensuous craving, thirst, wanting, etc.

Herewith is the exposition in conventional language of the Second Noble Truth as contained in the Thirteenth Sutta of the **Majjhima-Nikaya**:

"Truly, due to sensuous craving, conditioned through sensuous craving, entirely moved by sensuous craving, kings fight with kings, princes with princes, priests with priests, citizens with citizens; the mother quarrels with the son, the son with the father; brother quarrels with brother, brother with sister, sister with brother, friend with friend. Thus, given to dissension, quarrelling and fighting, they fall upon one another with fists, sticks, or weapons. And thereby they suffer death or deadly pain.

"And further, due to sensuous craving, conditioned through sensuous craving, impelled by sensuous craving, entirely moved by sensuous craving, people break into houses, rob, plunder, pillage whole houses, commit highway robbery, seduce the wives of others. Then, the rulers have such people caught, and inflict on them various forms of punishment. And thereby death or deadly pain. Now, this is the misery of sensuous craving, the heaping up of suffering in this present life, due to sensuous craving, conditioned through sensuous craving, caused by sensuous craving, entirely dependent on sensuous craving.

"And further, people take the evil way in deeds, the evil way in words, the evil way in thoughts; and by taking the evil way in deeds, words, and thoughts, at the dissolution of the body, after death, they fall into a downward state of existence, a state of suffering, into perdition, and the abyss of hell. But this is the misery of sensuous craving, the heaping up of suffering in the future life, due to sensuous craving, conditioned through sensuous craving, caused by sensuous craving, entirely dependent on sensuous craving."

"There is the sensual craving; the 'craving for (Eternal) Existence'; the 'craving for self-annihilation'.

'Sensual-craving' is the desire for the enjoyment of the five sense objects.

'Craving for existence' is the desire for continued, or eternal life, referring, in particular, to those higher worlds called fine-material and Immaterial Existence. It is closely connected with this so-called 'Eternity Belief' i.e. the belief in the absolute, eternal Ego-entity persisting independently of our body.

'Craving for Self-annihilation' (lit., for non-existence) is the outcome of the 'Belief in Annihilation' i.e. the delusive materialistic notion of a more or less real Ego, which is annihilated at death, and which does not stand in any causal relation with the time before death, and the time after death."

"The first two Truths are best explained through the Law of Dependent Origination, otherwise called Dependent Genesis. It has 12 Links or Nidanas, which are divided into 4 sections.

PAST	1. Ignorance 2. Karma Formations	Karma-Process 5 causes; 1, 2, 8, 9, 10.
PRESENT	3. Rebirth-Linking consciousness 4. Corporeality-Mentality 5. Six Bases 6. Impression 7. Feeling	Rebirth-Process 5 results: 3-7
PRESENT	8. Craving 9. Clinging 10. Process of Becoming	Karma-Process 5 causes: 1, 2, 8, 9, 10.
FUTURE	11. Rebirth 12. Old Age and Death	Rebirth-Process 5 Results: 3-7

From the above table, we see that
1. Ignorance
2. Karma Formations, or karma-Accumulations
3. Craving
4. Clinging
5. Process of Becoming of the past existence

produce

1. Rebirth-Linking Consciousness
2. Mentality and Corporeality
3. Six Bases
4. Impressions
5. Feeling

in the present existence. They are also called resultant mind and body (mentality and corporeality). They are the 5

57

resultant-Aggregates, and, being resultants, they do not produce results in future existences.

However, craving, clinging, becoming, ignorance and karma-formations in the present existence cause the resultant-Aggregates in the next existence. We have seen that these 5 Aggregates arise in a flash and immediately cease, and they keep on arising and ceasing without a break.

But it must be remembered that each unit of mentality-corporeality consists of Consciousness, Feeling, Perception, and Formations aggregates. The consciousness aggregate can be different all the time; it may be the eye-consciousness, or the auditory consciousness, and so on. The eye-consciousness has its own mental factors, though, as you know, seven mental factors that were first enumerated are universal, meaning they come into the composition of every mind. Similarly, with ear-consciousness and nose-consciousness and so on; the 7 universal mental factors always come into being but the other mental factors will be different.

As we get lower down in the several links of the chain, we see that the 5-causes beget Rebirth. Rebirth is inevitably followed by old age and death.

Now, Birth is suffering. This is a basic idea in Buddhism. Birth means arising, and all arising is suffering.

There are 2 types of suffering; normal suffering and abnormal suffering.

1. The arising of the 5-Aggregates is normal suffering. It is harmless suffering that even Arahats have to suffer; it has no moral force. It comprises all actions for the maintenance and preservation of the body and mind, such as, brushing one's teeth, satisfying hunger, earning one's livelihood, etc.

One cannot help the first kind of suffering and one has to be resigned to it.

2. The arising of the 5-Grasping Aggregates is abnormal suffering. We know how they arise, namely, by injecting the idea of 'I' or the arising of the Intoxicants, Cankers,

Biases, which in the final analysis are forms of craving. They are also called the Clinging Aggregates, begotten by attachment to the ordinary 5-Aggregates.

This is extra suffering because it is extra to the normal suffering of the 5-Aggregates. It is of the mind's own making. This extra suffering is called Causal suffering because it begets the harmless 5-Aggregates in a future existence. This begetting is called Birth, which we already know to be suffering.

This causal suffering leads to the continuation of rebirths. If causal suffering can be made to cease, as shown by the Buddha in the 4th Noble Truth of Suffering, we have cut the chain of existence.

To repeat, we must distinguish between the 5-resultant Aggregates and the 5-causal Aggregates; the latter arise because of causes made on the resultant Aggregates. What are these causes? They are the mental disturbances that arise after the 5-resultant aggregates have disappeared. When we recall the resultant aggregates, we may have anxiety, worry, fear, anger, sorrow, lamentation, grief, disappointment, disgust, dissatisfaction, discontent, distress, and so on. These mental disturbances are also called mental corruptions, fetters, etc. We know that according to the 1st Noble Truth, everything is suffering, and here we have causal suffering in this existence which will produce resultant suffering in the next existence.

We have seen that craving is the cause of suffering; when the object that is recalled is liked, it means that the craving for the object is satisfied. When the craving is not satisfied, there is dislike. Again there is this mental disturbance.

When we do not know what the resultant body and mind is, the mind goes on to cling to them or grasp them as 'I' or a person. Thus the idea 'I was born' arises and the further idea 'I do not want to be born again as life is troublesome'. The birth of such ideas is causal suffering which will produce results in a future existence.

Birth leads to decay and disease and death. With the clinging to the 5-Aggregates, there are such ideas as 'I do not want to grow old', 'I have disgust at being sick', and with the fear that sickness will lead to death there arise thoughts of 'I do not want to die'.

Also there are ideas that you do not want to be separated from your loved ones or you do not want to be associated with persons that are not dear to you. There arise dislike and disgust. There also arise fear and worry and anxiety and disappointment and frustration.

All this is causal suffering due to grasping and clinging to the 5-Aggregates. There is disturbance of the mind that 'I' is going to get sick or die. The mind is disturbed, when actually the person, taken as the object of recall, is imaginary. Your imaginary object brings on fear and anxiety and envy and jealousy, etc.

These are the arisings of fetters and cankers and hindrances. All this is due to unwise thinking which is thinking not in accordance with the 4-Noble Truths.

The resultant aggregates arise and cease all the time, and it is only occasionally that we recall the resultant aggregates and have good or bad reactions, and it is these reactions that are the cause of suffering and will produce results in future existences.

It is all a question of needs versus wants. The human body needs to be looked after; you have to brush your teeth and keep the body clean and protect it from the weather; you have to eat to satisfy hunger, and take exercise, and take medicine in time of sickness, and earn sufficient money through work. These are some of the needs; it is the resultant body and mind that produce the needs.

On the other hand, the mind has the wants, the desires, the craving, for this and that. There arise the mental disturbances of which we have spoken earlier.

We have to understand that craving is the cause of all the suffering, and this craving is subjective. The mental reactions that arise on the satisfaction or non-satisfaction of the craving are in our own mind and it is not the fault of external happenings, etc.

We want to control other people, we want to control events, and we want to control things, and because our wants are not satisfied, there is causal suffering. The answer is to control our mental reactions. A few examples will make the point clear.

Birth is inexorably followed by decay and death; it is an inevitable process and cannot be prevented by anyone or any agency. You do not want decay and death; you do not want to die. Not wanting all this is the cause of causal suffering, which produces resultant suffering in the next existence. When there is decay and death, you get sorrow and lamentation and misery and grief and despair. If you accept decay and death with equanimity, you will not have your bad reactions. Your reactions are subjective and could be controlled. You are not at peace. **Mea culpa. Mea culpa.** (It's my own fault, It's my own fault.)

You lose your watch, and you suspect someone. However, it is of small value and you say to yourself that you have not lost anything of appreciable value. You have no bad reactions and you accept the loss with equanimity. But if the price of the watch is somewhat high, and you have craving arising, it will cause evil reactions towards the suspected thief. You cannot control your craving and you have ideas of revenge and similar bad reactions. If you can accept the loss with equanimity, you will have mental peace; otherwise your mental craving will cause you untold suffering. **Mea culpa. Mea culpa.**

It rains. You have, however, made arrangements to go out on a picnic. It does not matter to you that the rain is very good for the farmers of the country-side. You want to enjoy yourself. Your sense of enjoyment has been thwarted; your craving, your thirst is for your enjoyment. The mental reaction to the rain is one of anger, disappointment, disgust. All these are mental disturbances; these disturbances are subjective. If you did not have these bad mental reactions, based on your selfish craving, there would be peace within you. It is not the event outside that is at fault; the fault is in your selfish mental reactions. **Mea culpa. Mea culpa.**

Dinner is served. You go to the table and find that you do not like the food. You call up the cook and scold him or her. Maybe you will fist him or her. You **want** to enjoy good food. Your mental reaction to the bad cooking is subjective. The external circumstance, namely, the cook is blamed. Actually it is your craving for good food or good enjoyment that has caused the mental reaction which has led to the scolding or the fisting of the cook. If you had not had this craving, your mental reactions would not have been bad. The fault lies with you and not with the cook. If you had not developed these bad emotions, you would have been at peace. **Mea culpa. Mea culpa.**

You go to a restaurant. There is a delicacy on the table. You like it. Your craving is satisfied for the moment, for you **want** to enjoy good food. Your mental reaction is that when you come to this restaurant the next time you must order this delicacy, for your mental reaction is satisfaction. But supposing that this delicacy had not been to your taste, though it might have pleased the rest of those with you, you have a mental reaction of disgust or anger or disappointment and you say to yourself that you will never come to this restaurant again, regardless of how it strikes your relatives or friends. Your craving has not been satisfied. If you had been able to prevent these bad reactions, your mind would have been at peace. **Mea culpa. Mea culpa.**

You hear that someone has made an ill remark about you. Your craving or wanting is that he should have made a good remark about you. You have thoughts of anger or maybe even revenge against him. It is this non-fulfilment of your craving that causes all these bad reactions. Without these bad reactions you would be at peace. If he were a good friend, or you considered him a good friend of yours, your reactions would be very strong and you would think of revenge and all that. So everything depends on your reactions to what you have heard. Without these reactions, which are subjective, you would be at peace. **Mea culpa. Mea culpa.**

You have a resultant body as the result of the actions of your past existences. You must expect some sort of pain sometimes. Not wanting this pain produces causal suffering; you do not want this pain and you have evil reactions towards the matter. You cannot suffer the pain with equanimity, namely without your bad reactions, which are subjective. **Mea culpa. Mea culpa.**

3RD NOBLE TRUTH

The 3rd Noble Truth says that the cessation of craving is the cessation of suffering. It is as simple as that.
The cessation of Craving is Peace. It is Nirvana.
The Buddha says that there is an Unborn, Unoriginated, Uncreated, Unformed. If there were not this Unborn, this Unoriginated, this Uncreated, this Unformed, escape from the world of the born, the originated, the created, the formed would not be possible.
But since there is an Unborn, Unoriginated, Uncreated, Unformed, therefore is escape possible from the world of the born, the originated, the created, the formed?
Some authors have translated the above four words as 'Unborn, unbecome, unmade, unconditioned'. The main meaning is that everything, except Nirvana, is conditioned, which means that the conditioned is created by mundane causes and therefore is not free from ageing and death. It is only reachable by the Path which is the 4th Noble Truth; it is reachable but not arousable, for it exists from the very beginning.
A person who has no craving at all will certainly be at peace. Let us study the following fraction:

$$\frac{\text{desires fulfilled}}{\text{sum total of desires}}$$

If for example the denominator, namely, the sum total of desires, is 100, and the numerator, namely, the desires fulfilled, is 40, you have the fraction $\frac{40}{100}$ or 40 per cent fulfilled. You will still be unhappy because of desires that are not yet fulfilled.

If however you reduce the quantum of desires, if you reduce the denominator to 90, you get the fraction $\frac{40}{90}$. If you reduce your desires to 50, you have the fraction $\frac{40}{50}$, which represents the fulfillment of 80 per cent of your desires.

If you reduce your desires to 40, you get $\frac{40}{40}$ or complete happiness.

Nirvana is sometimes described as the signless State. This can be illustrated by the idea of the clinical thermometer that is used to measure the temperature of the body when there is fever. This fever may be brought on by several causes, such as influenza, malaria, etc. We use the clinical thermometer when we have fever, but when the fever is absent, we normally are content to let things be.

Now, craving is mental fever. We have seen that these mental disturbances are causal suffering. Craving is the one and only cause that brings on mental fever, and the 4 Noble Truths are the only thermometer for measuring the temperature of the Mind. Craving can be very subtle and refined, when there will be only a slight mental fever, but when the craving is coarse there is an appreciable fever.

We are so used to taking objects that are external to ourselves. It is said that the mind inclines towards an object. Have we ever tried to recall the mind that sees these objects? Instead of recalling the object, we should recall the mind that saw the object.

If you look inwards at any moment, you will observe the subjective mind. At this very moment as you are reading this book, you are not disturbed by any craving and the mind is at peace. Actually, this peace has been there all the time. You have not caused it to happen but you have just noticed it. This is peace and you experience it when you look inwards.

Look inwards at any instant of time and you will exerience Peace. Of course, during the day when you are awake and you go through the different experiences of the day and carry on the work of earning a living or meeting friends, and so on, it is not necessary for craving to arise.

Whenever there is no craving, there is no mental fever and no mental corruptions.

We know that the characteristic nature of the mind is to know or be aware of an object. The process of knowing a thing is an impersonal process. There is knowing of an object but no one who knows owns that knowing. Something is known and that is all. Pay attention to the knowing of it.

One is so used to looking outwards but if we were to stop looking outwards and look inwards, the mind playing its own impersonal operations of knowing or calling up ideas, only then will one really come to know oneself.

We have to observe the subjective mental States. For example, while one is reading, try to look inwards. The words are taken as the object and let there be no criticism about the ideas made by the words. The mind is not thinking of external matters. Mental corruptions are absent which means craving is also absent, and when craving is absent, there is the signless, absolute, timeless and infinite Nirvana.

Nirodha Sacca is another Truth. When there is no cause, there is no effect.

The 2nd Noble Truth says that craving is the cause of suffering and it is called **Samudaya Sacca**. Craving is the cause, and suffering is the effect; when there is the cause, there is the effect.

When there is no cause, there is no effect; this is also a Truth. It is the 3rd Noble Truth, called **Nirodha Sacca**.

In Insight Meditation, first it is the Insight consciousness. At the **Gotrabu** stage, there is the change of lineage when the mind of the worldling changes automatically to that of the Noble One. It changes from Insight consciousness to Path Consciousness.

Insight consciousness is accompanied by the ordinary mind constituents plus the 5 dominant ones of Wisdom, Faith, Diligence, Mindfulness and Concentration. They are also called **Bala** (Powers).

In the 8-fold Noble Path, they go by other names and other guises, but they are included.

THE 4TH NOBLE TRUTH

The 4th Noble Truth is the Noble 8-fold Path, sometimes called the Noble Eight Constituent Path.

It consists of the following 8 mental constituents:

1. Right Understanding } Wisdom
2. Right Thought

3. Right Speech
4. Right Action } Morality
5. Right Livelihood

6. Right Effort
7. Right Mindfulness } Concentration
8. Right Concentration

They are mental accompaniments that accompany Path Consciousness. They have been translated differently by different authors, and so it is best to learn the Pali names, so that there is no mistake as to what is meant.

They are supramundane as Nirvana is taken as the object. When we use the expression that Nirvana is taken as the object, it means that this 3rd Noble Truth which is Nirvana, is taken as the object by the states of the 4th Noble Truth, the 8 mental states of the Noble Eightfold Path. The Mind does not take other external objects but it is looking inwards with Nirvana as the object, and there is Peace. This is the practice of the Noble Eightfold Path.

We know that craving is not caused by external sources but it is internal; craving is subjective. We have to see that it does not arise and we are then at peace.

Mindfulness is required to look inwards and that is the meaning of Right Mindfulness which is one of the factors of the Noble 8-fold Path.

We have seen that birth inevitably produces decay and death. You do not want to die, and there is sorrow and lamentation and suffering and grief and anguish, and this again produces ignorance and karma-accumulations and once again the next round of existence.

The 4 Noble Truths

This ignorance has been called the ignorance of the 4 Noble Truths. Once we really know and understand the 4 Noble Truths, as they should be known, we will prevent future births. It is therefore imperative that we practise the 4 Noble Truths, including the practice of the 8-fold Noble Path, in order to achieve our goal of stoppage of future births.

The Path is divided into Higher Morality, Higher Mentality, and Higher Wisdom.

A smoker has the practice of smoking. He has his cigarettes and cigars and his pipe and his lighter and matches. The practice is apparent.

A non-smoker does not smoke. He has the practice of non-smoking. Similarly in the 8-fold Noble Path, he has the practice of non-craving.

This 4th Noble Truth is **Magga Sacca**. Path Wisdom comes in a flash. It knows all the 4 Noble Truths simultaneously.

Part Two
Meditation

Chapter 6
Right Understanding

Buddhist Practice begins with Right Understanding, otherwise called Right Views, and ends with Right Understanding of a higher stage.

This Chapter gives food for meditation, and meditation is always with knowledge. Buddhism is a religion of action, and there is no time to waste.

The Buddha renounced his kingdom in order to solve the problem of Birth and Death. There is Death because of the arising of Birth.

As soon as we awake, the idea of Self begins. The 6-Door Machine begins to work. We cognise the outside world through the 6 Doors.

We all want pleasure and pleasurable feelings all the time. However, these pleasures cloy and turn to suffering.

The 5-Aggregates arise. They flash forth but are evanescent. They appear and disappear, arise and cease. They are **Sankhāra**, one of the meanings of which is Formed, Compounded, Conditioned. It is the same as **Sankhata**, and comprises all phenomena of existence.

Only sometimes arise the 6-Grasping Aggregates when there is unwise thinking, and produce mental suffering, like worry, grief, anxiety, etc. This is causal suffering and causes future existences. We must ensure the cessation of causal suffering at the stage of Craving in order to stop future existences. This is done by Insight Meditation.

In Insight Meditation, we must know the difference between ultimates and concepts. There are 82 ultimates, each having its own individual essence.

In Insight Meditation,
1. There must be knowledge of the ultimates of Mind and Matter, each having its individual essence;
2. We must know the cause and effect of the arising and ceasing of these ultimates;
3. We must know Impermanence, Suffering and No-Self with reference to these ultimates.

Eventually, we get Path Wisdom, leading to Nirvana.

The first step is to become a Stream-Entrant, which means the elimination of the Wrong View Self.

The Doctrine of **Anatta** can be understood as composed of 3 parts:
1. there is no soul,
2. there is no self,
3. there is no control over our body processes.

The human body does not exist in terms of **ultimates**; it is on a par with the statement in conventional truth that water exists, but water does not exist in terms of ultimate truth, that is, in reality. The Law of **Anatta** says that the human body carries out its bodily functions automatically and we have no control over it, and there is no need to put a Self into it.

Once the Buddha understood that everything in this world was **Anatta** and that there was no creator, he developed an independence of Mind that was unique in the history of human thought.

The 2nd Noble Truth says that Craving is the cause of Suffering. Craving is a Mind Constituent and arises along with Consciousness. Only when Consciousness arises can Craving arise. Craving no longer arises with an Arahat, but with ordinary persons, Craving arises occasionally. As Craving arises with Consciousness, it is momentary and fleeting, but when it does arise, it creates havoc.

Craving arises because of ignorance of the 4 Noble Truths. Arahats know the 4 Noble Truths and they have practised them to perfection. Stream-Entrants know the 4 Noble Truths but they have not practised them to perfection.

Buddha says that everything is **anatta**. This doctrine is uniquely his.

When **anatta** is realised, there is no more attachment to self. There is detachment from the 5-Aggregates.

In Western parlance, if we carry on a conversation and, say, are embarrassed, or do not like the trend of the conversation, we change the subject. In Abhidhamma, the same thing is called changing the object.

Most Meditation Centres begin with concentration on **conceptual** objects but they never seem to get beyond this point. Ordinarily you contemplate on **conceptual** objects, like charity, precepts and concentration.

Some meditation centres start you on Insight practices of meditating on the individual essences of the Conceptual objects, of which there are so many. But they go no further.

But when you do Insight-meditation in your body and contemplate on the arising and cessation of the 5-Aggregates, you come to 'see' the 3 characteristics of **anicca, dukkha** and **anatta**.

You 'see' or are aware of the 3 characteristics in 3 different ways, namely, by Consciousness, Perception, and Wisdom.

Firstly, is respect of awareness by Consciousness. In the beginning it is **Eye-Consciousness** which is aware of just the seeing, or **Ear-Consciousness** which is aware of just the hearing, and so on. Then comes automatically mind-consciousness: first is **mano-dhatu** followed by **mano-vinnana**.

Secondly, is respect of awareness by Perception. **Perception just marks and notes**; it marks and notes the 3 characteristics of the 5-Aggregates.

Thirdly, is respect of awareness by Wisdom. Wisdom can know everything in the 31 planes of existence. It knows how the Eye Consciousness arises and Ear Consciousness arises, etc. It knows how Mind-Consciousness arises. It knows the intrinsic essences of the elements, that water is H_2O. It knows Contact, Feeling and all the other 50 mind-constituents separately. It knows how the 5-Aggregates arise and cease. It knows the **anicca, dukkha** and **anatta** of the 5-Aggregates. It knows that Eye-Consciousness arises only if there is a sensitive-eye. If there is a defective sensitive-eye or if the eye is closed, there is no sensitive-eye in actuality and there can be no mind-consciousness that would have arisen through eye-consciousness. (There can, however, be a mind-consciousness arising through other sense-objects or mental-objects.) It knows that ear-consciousness arises only if there is a sensitive-ear in actuality. Again, if there is a defective sensitive-ear, there can be no ear-consciousness and no mind-consciousness arising therefrom. And so on with the other sense organs which must not be defective.

And therefore, you see that it is only through Wisdom that we reach our goal. So it is imperative that wisdom should arise, but it arises only through knowledge. Without knowledge, there can be no wisdom.

So you can see that Perception which marks and notes will not lead to wisdom. A life time spent just perceiving will not lead to wisdom.

Nor will consciousness without knowledge turn to wisdom.

Then there is the question of the existence of a Soul (**atta**) or Self or 'I'. Because of the belief in **atta**, there have been milleniums and aeons of existences in the 31 planes of existence.

Now, how does this idea of 'I' arise? You speak of 'I see', 'I hear', 'I smell', etc. You use the word 'I' every time there is a thought.

Actually, it is citta that sees, and hears, and smells, etc. Only when there is a citta does the idea of 'I' arise.

When there is no citta, no idea of 'I' arises. We can then ask the question, is citta 'I'? Most people will say that citta is 'I'. There is anger because of the idea of 'I'. There is worry because of the idea of 'I'. There is everything because of the idea of 'I'. But if there is no citta, no idea of 'I', soul, or atta or self arises. So can there be an atta, or soul or 'I'? We also confuse mind-consciousness with 'I', or soul, or self or atta. But if there is no citta, there can be no mind-consciousness, because mind-consciousness cannot arise without eye-consciousness, ear-consciousness, etc., or a mental-object (**Dhamma-arammana**). For a mind-consciousness arises only if there is a cause. Therefore it cannot be an atta, or soul, or self or 'I'. Accordingly there can be no soul or atta or self or 'I'.

In the 31 planes of existence, there is craving for sensual pleasures, craving for existence and craving for annihilation of existence. The idea of soul or self or 'I' or atta arises because of these three beliefs. You have wandered a lot in the 31 planes of existence because of this idea of soul, self, atta, or 'I', because of Ignorance which begets karma production which begets the germinal force.

The germinal force in this existence ripens and dies, causing a fresh germinal force in the next existence, like the chicken and the egg in a non-ending series. It is this germinal force that separates the species and individuals of the species in plants and animals and humans and entities in the 31 planes of existence.

If you do **samatha-concentration** and reach a certain level of proficiency, you can see the arising and re-arising of these germinal forces.

And you realise the Suffering in all these existences, for all existence and life is Suffering.

But luckily the Buddha taught that there is a release from birth and death and suffering. By practising Right Understanding, you achieve **anatta**-wisdom. After achieving **anatta**-

wisdom you are left only with the needs of the Ego-entity or personality or the 5-Aggregates, and no more with its wants. There is no more new existence, and you are free from Craving of all kinds. And there is no more suffering. You are off the wheel of existence.

There are many aspects of Right-Understanding. One aspect is that beings are the owners of their own karma.

Another aspect arises from a full comprehension of the 3 characteristics of **anicca, dukkha and anatta** of the 5-Aggregates.

Another aspect is the Insight-wisdom-Right-Understanding arising from perception with Insight-wisdom.

And finally the supramundane-Path-Fruition-Right-Understanding arising from the attainment of the Holy Paths and Fruition thereof.

You get Insight-wisdom with the 5 dominant mind constituents of wisdom, faith, diligence, mindfulness and Concentration.

Then you go beyond Insight-consciousness. You get to Path-Consciousness with the 8 mind-constituents of the Noble Eightfold Path.

You see Nirvana. The Path-Consciousness merges into Nirvana. Nirvana, incidentally, is not inside you but outside you.

The benefit of following the Buddha's teaching is that it produces Peace, the Peace that passeth all Understanding.

Though this book deals with ultimates, we must remember that we live in a molecular world. All manifestation is in terms of molecules, but we must not forget the ultimate constitution of molecules, namely the atoms and atomic particles.

Every aggregation is molecular and therefore pannatti. We see atoms and atomic particles with the inner eye, but life exists only as molecules.

Descartes said, "cogito, ergo sum", meaning, "I think, therefore I am". He does not explain what is meant by "I", "think" or "I am".

However, Abhidhamma explains all this and more. It explains how consciousness arises, how mind is consciousness plus something, etc., etc.

"I" is the personalisation of consciousness, mind, or thought; these three words are used synonymously for Citta in the Abhidhamma.

As for "think", the processes of thought, the courses of cognition, are explained in detail in the Abhidhamma.

"I am" means the 5-Aggregates, the Personality.

If we want to get at the Truth, we must know what Citta is. Citta is a paramatta and cannot be "I", which is pannatti. Therefore, when we do Vipassana Meditation, it must be done on paramatta and not on pannatti.

If we meditate on pannatti objects, we must get merit in the worlds of kama, rupa and arupa, but it does lead to the stage of Sotapanna which leads to Magga Wisdom and to Nirvana.

We must know how consciousness arises. Consciousnesses arise through the 6-Doors, namely, 1. visual consciousness, 2. auditory consciousness, 3. sound consciousness, 4. smell consciousness, 5. taste consciousness, and 6. mind consciousness.

They arise when there is conjunction with an object, namely, visual object, auditory object, sound object, etc. And thus arises awareness of an object.

What is the "I" with reference to the Mind? "I" can be deemed to be the "Agent" of the Mind. If that be so, whose "Agent" is the Mind? The answer is that Mind is the "Agent" of the 5 Aggregates.

In Vipassana Meditation, we are meditating on the 5 Aggregates. And therefore we must know how and why the 5 Aggregates arise, and the characteristics of each Aggregate.

There are 5-Aggregates in all.
When consciousness arises,
1. there arises citta and cetasikas, and the citta-produced Aggregate, which is the Materiality Aggregate.

2. vinnana or consciousness Aggregate;
3. vedana or feeling Aggregate.
4. sanna or perception Aggregate.
5. sankhara Aggregate of willing and striving with the remainder of the 50 cetasika.

In the mundane world you use sati (mindfulness), viriya (effort or diligence), panna (wisdom) all the time to get all your successes.

Similarly, in the supramundane world, it is sati, viriya, panna in its supramundane forms.

As we get on with Vipassana Meditation, we come eventually to Magga Wisdom and the Nirvanic Peace which passeth all Understanding.

Buddha taught the Truth. He taught the Truth in line with a succession of Buddhas. He taught the truth of Birth and Death. He taught the truth of Dukkha (suffering), and how to get out of this Samsara. That's the Goal, namely, freedom from Rebirth.

With the First Sermon, millions and millions of Devas and Brahmas achieved Freedom from Rebirth. So, also when he preached the Second Sermon. No more the arising of the 5-Aggregates in the 31 planes of Existence.

It is a great thought to be liberated at last. After having been once a King, once a slave, once a rich man, and once a poor man, once a deva, once in purgatory and a non-ending series of rebirths, at long last, Freedom from Rebirth.

As soon as there is birth, any where and every where, there begins this round of Dukkha. It is just dukkha and dukkha.

I for one would not relish the idea of being reborn into this world for all is dukkha.

Similarly, in the other planes of existence. There may be temporary snatches of so-called happiness (sukkha), for example, when doing jhana, but it is basically always dukkhas and always back to purgatory.

The universe is molecular. It is mundane. But we are now dealing with the supramundane. One should not mix up the two.

Then come glimmerings of Freedom from the wheel of existence. Freedom from Rebirth.

After attaining to Nirvana, and before one's demise, what sort of existence does one lead? One must understand that this is a world of pannatti.

What sort of existence did the Buddha lead? He could possibly have some annoyance or anger but without any craving, or some pleasures of taste, etc., without any craving.

And before we ourselves become arahats, we could practise staying without any craving. During that time, we would be at peace. It would be an exciting life.

And thus may Buddha's teaching lead to Freedom from Rebirth for all in this Universe, for all in this World-System and all other World-Systems.

Chapter 7
Vipassanā Meditation

The purpose of **Vipassanā** Meditation is to become a Sotapañña in the first instance, the first of the Noble Ones, and then go on to the Second and Third Stages, culminating in becoming an Arahat. The method is to discover and penetrate into the actually existing ultimate realities, both of matter and mind, and to arrive at the **anicca, dukkha, anatta** characteristics of your 5-Aggregates. This leads to the different steps of **Vipassanā** Wisdom right up to the stage of **Magga** and **Phala** Wisdom and to Nirvana, the **Summum Bonum** of Buddhism.

It is at the stage of **Gotrabhu** that the **Vipassanā citta** is automatically changed to that of **Magga citta**. It is the change of lineage from that of a worldling and you become a Noble One.

The **vipassanā citta** has a complement of 34 **cetasikas**, including the 5 dominant Powers (**balas**) of **paññā, saddha, viraya, sati,** and **samādhi**. It has only 34 because the 3 Abstinences are counted as one, as only one of the 3 functions, whenever called upon to function, two of them being always idle.

The **Magga citta** also has its full complement of 36 **cetasikas**, including the 8 **cetasikas** of the 8-fold Noble Path.

Eventually you break the chain of causation, and you are on the 'other shore', having left the Wheel of Existence.

It is only on the basis of the knowledge of the ultimates that final **vipassanā** wisdom can be obtained. For example, meditation on the **anicca, dukkha, anatta** characteristics of conventional things (**paññatti**) cannot produce **Magga** wisdom.

Suppose two lawyers were arguing before a Judge, all of them learned in the law, and one lawyer is making his legal points. His lawyer opponent is listening carefully, and all of a sudden he gets a flash of legal wisdom to counter the other lawyer's argument. The legal wisdom cannot come without a knowledge of the law. Similarly when you meditate with **Vipassana** knowledge, you get a flash of supra-mundane or transcendental wisdom.

Vipassana is the study of cause and effect. It is essential that one be able to make a proper differentiation between **paramattha** (ultimate realities) and **paññatti** (concepts, ideas, terms, etc): otherwise one will unknowingly fall into the trap of 'meditation' on **Paññatti**.

There are 16 steps in **Vipassanā** Meditation:

1. **Nāma-Rūpa Pariccheda Ñāna**, being the knowledge arrived at by dissecting Mind and Body into their ultimate parts.
2. **Pacaya Parigaha Ñāna**, being the knowledge of the arisings and ceasings, being cause and effect.
3. **Samma-Sana Ñāna**, being the knowledge of the arising and ceasings of the past, future and present.
4. **Udaya-vaya-nuppassanā-Ñāna**, knowledge which reflects on the rise and fall of the 5-Aggregates through the 6-doors.
5. **Bhanga-nupassanā-Ñāna**, knowledge which reflects on the breaking up or perishable nature of the 5-Aggregates.
6. **Bhayat-uppathanā-Ñāna**, knowledge of the defects of the 5-Aggregates.
7. **Adinava-nupassanā-Ñāna**, knowledge which reflects on the dangers of the 5-Aggregates.

8. Nibbida-nupassanā-Ñāna, knowledge which reflects on the feeling of disgust aroused by the 5-Aggregates.
9. Muncitu-kamyata-Ñāna, knowledge of the desire for release from the 5-Aggregates which arouse feelings of disgust.
10. Pati-sankha-nupassanā-Ñāna, knowledge which reflects on the detailed analysis of the 5-Aggregates in order to be released from them.
11. Sankha-ruppekkha-Ñāna, knowledge of indifference towards the 5-Aggregates.
12. Anuloma-Ñāna, Adaptive knowledge which arises in connection with the 4 Noble Truths.
13. Gotrabhu-Ñāna, change of lineage of the consciousness that arises.
14. Magga-Ñāna, burst of Wisdom that we are seeking.
15. Phala-Ñāna, fruition-consciousness.
16. Pacca-vekkhana-Ñāna, the post-Phala Meditation on Magga, Phala, and Nirvana.

In your own body, and in another's body, find out and penetrate into the actual existing phenomena.

1. The realities are **paramattha**.
2. Non-realities exist as **sammuti** truth. It is ordinary usage in conventional terms, like, man, woman, person, 'I', a breathing body showing continuity; it is **paññatti**.

My body is the manifestation of the 4-Mahā-Bhūtas (Primaries). They are bound together as one.

Meditate to ferret out the individual essences of
    1. **Pathavī** – hardness, softness.
    2. **Āpo** – coherence, inherence, growth.
    3. **Tejo** – heat (and absence of heat), and
    4. **Vāyo** – Motion or resistance to motion, hardening with air-pressure

Find out in your body, consisting of from the top of the head down to your toes, the facts of heat and cold, where cold is the lessening of heat.

Know that the manifestations of heat and cold, its individual essence, has no form or entity.

a. **Tejo.** Heat. Practise finding out heat and cold. It is rūpa (matter), and its changeability is the essence of matter.
b. **Vāyo.** Motion or resistance to motion. Find out in your body, motion, and resistance to motion. Know that changeability is the essence of matter.
c. **Āpo.** Find out in your body the growth and the linking together of the 4 Primaries. Āpo is coherence, inherence, fluidity. Remember that changeability is the essence of matter.
d. **Pathavī.** All the other 3 Primaries are based on Pathavī, namely, heat, motion and resistance to motion, coherence and liquidity. Know the individual essences and the characteristics of hardness and softness, know that it is constantly changing (transient).

Thus in every way, from top to bottom, and sideways left and right, know that changeability is the essence of matter (rūpa).

Then, along with the 4 Primaries, are the 4 derived qualities or properties, all arising and disappearing together:

a. colour
b. smell
c. taste
d. nutriment.

It is the Octad, all arising together. Add jīvita (psychic life) to the Octad, and we get the nonad. Add the sensitive parts of the organs which are the fruition of past karma, namely, depending on past karma. It is the decad.

There are millions of such decad cells, all with ākāsa (space) in between.

Your whole body, outside and inside, is composed of these cells, of which you must know their essence severally.
Octad + jīvita = nonad
With visual pasāda (sensitive eye) we have one kind of cell.
With hearing pasāda, we have another kind of cell.
With smell pasāda, we have another kind of cell.
With taste pasāda, another kind of cell.
With body pasāda, another kind of cell.
With heart pasāda, (hādaya-vatthu), another kind of cell. It must be noted, however, that Abhidhamma denies the existence of the physical hādaya-vatthu.

So once again, in your body, high and low, and sideways, know that changeability is the essence of matter. They are all changeable essences, and not person or creature, nor 'I', nor man, nor woman.

Practice regarding the arising of Nāma

Taking heat as your object, 4 kinds of Nāma Aggregates arise. One Aggregate knows, one feels, one notes, and one strives.

With body base, there arises body consciousness. In the feeling of heat, there is vedanā; there is feeling of different kinds, pleasurable or otherwise, and you note (saññā). In the feeling, which is of different kinds, you have to strive continually to keep it arising; this is sankhāra aggregate.

These 4 aggregates arise together; they are the 4 Nāma aggregates.

(NOTE) : If there were only one, it would amount to atta, the admission of atta. There is nothing in the world that exists just by itself singly. There is no atta.

Along with the 4 nāma aggregates, there arises Mind-produced matter. It arises and disappears; it is transient, which is the essence of matter. Thus we have one aggregate for Body and 4 aggregates for Mind, making 5 Aggregates.

Everytime you see, remember, recall, note, know nāma-rupa. Meditate on the fact, and be mindful of it.

Everytime you smell, meditate similarly.

Everytime you taste, do similarly.

Abhidhamma

Everytime you **touch**, do similarly.
Everytime you **know**, do similarly.

Thus, a meditator meditates on his body and on another's body, and knows that, except for the 5-Aggregates, there is no person or being or 'I', or man or woman.
The aim is to know reality by severally dissecting its parts.

1. This is **Nāma-Rūpa Pariccheda wisdom**

In the wink of an eye, in a flash of lightning, during that period called **khana**, there is **uppatti** (arising), **thi** (decay) and **bin** (ceasing).

Life of Nāma
Nāma exists for the 3 small **khanas** of arising, decay and ceasing. For one unit of **rupa** ceasing, there are 17 units of nāma ceasing.

Rūpa and **Nāma** are conditioned and therefore cannot be only one unit. The old gives place to the new. The new are arising all the time, and it appears as if there is one continuous appearing.

When you are doing **Vipassanā** Meditation and you do not achieve **Nāma Rūpa Pariccheda Wisdom**, it will be an impediment to understanding the characteristic marks of **Anicca, Dukkha** and **Anatta**.

There are so many rūpas.
1. Basic 4 **Mahā-Bhūtas** (Primaries), arising in the whole body.
2. Derived from the 4 Primaries, are the 4:
    colour
    smell
    taste
    nutriment
3. a. **Jīvita rūpa** that gives life to the body
   b. Feminity
   c. Masculinity
   d. Body **Pasāda**

The above 12 are for the whole body.

4. Sensitive Eye
   Sensitive ear
   Sensitive nose
   Sensitive tongue
   Sensitive body (hādaya-vatthu)
   Sound rūpa — occasionally arises with belly, throat, mouth, tongue, lips.

They lead to the idea of person, 'I'.

These 18 rupas make this body, which has no sentience.

'Seeing', knowing visual form, depending on the sensitive eye;
'Hearing', knowing sound, depending on the sensitive ear;
'Smelling', knowing smell, dependent on the sensitive nose.
'Tasting', knowing taste, dependent on the sensitive tongue.
'Touching', knowing touch, dependent on the sensitive body.
'Knowing', dependent on the hādaya-vatthu, or heart base.
These 6 'knowings' are due to the taking of an object.

Understand that Nāma and Rūpa do not mix; they are separate, and should be thus meditated on. The 6 'knowings' are Nāma, and the 6 doors are rūpa.

Meditate on this intermittently.

There are 18 rūpas on which you do not meditate.

2. Paccaya-parigaha-Nāma

   Generators of Matter:
   1. Karma
   2. Citta
   3. Utu
   4. Āhāra

Karma means the past good and bad karma, which started with the birth (patisandi) consciousness, and causes the karma-produced rūpa to arise; it is the seed of the rūpa.

Citta, starting after the patisandi consciousness, starting with the first bhavanga, causes the citta-produced rūpa to arise.

Utu causes both the internal and external body-formations.

Āhāra causes the internal and external rūpas to arise.

Arising of 4 Nāma Aggregates

Eye pasāda (sensitive eye) + visual object + light + manasikāra cause to arise visual consciousness, and thus the 4 Nāma Aggregates arise.

Sensitive ear + sound + medium + manasikāra produce auditory consciousness and the 4 Nāma Aggregates.

Sensitive nose + smell + air + manasikāra produce smell consciousness.

Sensitive Tongue, etc. Similar.

Sensitive Body, etc. Similar.

Mental pasada + mental base + mental object produce mental consciousness and the 4 Nāma-Aggregates.

Along with the 4 Nāma-Aggregates arises citta-produced matter, making the 5th Aggregate. So each of the 5 Aggregates arises and ceases.

The knowing of the arisings and ceasings, being cause and effect, is **Paccaya-Parigaha** Wisdom.

3. Samma-Sana Wisdom

Meditate on the arising and cessation of the 5-Aggregates in the past. Meditate on each singly and severally, with reference to the **Anicca, Dukkha** and **Anatta** characteristics of existence. They arose because of the 6-Doors.

Similarly for the present arisings and cessations, similarly for the future arisings and cessations.

These 5-Aggregates are no good at all. They arise and disappear all the time, and you cannot depend on them at all. Each of the following eleven distinctions of these aggregates is no good, and they appear and disappear similarly.

1. In the past, they arose and disappeared. They have the characteristics of **anicca, dukkha** and **anatta**, and therefore are no good at all.

2. In the future, they will arise and disappear and have the 3 characteristics of **anicca, dukkha** and **anatta**.

3. In the present, they are no good at all. They are arising and disappearing all the time, having the 3 characteristics of existence.
4. Externally, also, the 5-Aggregates of animals, etc., are arising and disappearing all the time, bearing the 3 characteristics.
5. Internally, also, they are no good, having the 3 characteristics.
6. They can be coarse. All these 5-Aggregates are bad. If there is arising of dosa, one has to be afraid.
7. They can be refined, and all are bad. They give the idea of getting you merit and that this will get you to the abodes of the Devas. Thus you are induced, for instance, to build a monastery. They induce you to make charity (dāna) and keep the precepts (sīla), promising Kāma Kusala (merit) and rūpa kusala and arūpa kusala, when actually these kusalas are anicca, dukka and anatta. These 5-Aggregates are not dependable at all. They are bad.
8. They can be of the inferior kind, and full of lobha, dosa and moha.
9. They can be of the superior kind, but they are not dependable, replete with the 3 characteristics of anicca, dukkha and anatta.
10. They can be of the distant kind. One can visualise them existing far away but they all exhibit the 3 characteristics, and are no good.
11. They can be of the near kind, but they exhibit the 3 characteristics.

4. Udaya-vaya-nupassanā-ñāna

From now, we stick to the present, and no more of the past and future. This applies to this and the remaining stages.

Udaya means arising, and
vaya means cessation.

We meditate on the arising and ceasing of the 5-Aggregates. They arise through the 6-Doors which are located all over the body. They arise from different causes, through the sensitive eye, the sensitive ear, sensitive nose, etc., at different doors, and after arising, they immediately disappear just where they had arisen at the different localities of the body.

The arising and ceasing shows their **anicca** quality, meaning not permanent.

5. Bhanga

As you meditate, the arising and ceasing of the 5-Aggregates become fast, so fast, you will not see the arising but only the ceasing, just as you see the crumbling of a house built on the very edge of a river.

You will realise that craving or wanting anything produces suffering. For example, you engage a servant. Later, he lets you down and there is a theft and you have to go to Court. You come to realise that because you **wanted** a servant, you got trouble and suffering.

This craving causes the 5-Grasping Aggregates to arise and the result is suffering.

Another example. You want to eat a particular thing. Someone comes and gives you this particular thing. You eat and get unwell. You see that the **wanting** to eat that thing is the cause of your trouble, your suffering. You see the cause and effect.

You see that attachment to the 5-Aggregates is bad, because the attachment or craving causes the arising of the 5-Grasping Aggregates, and thus you realise that suffering is caused.

From this stage of mental development onwards, you come to realise that suffering results because of your **wanting** anything, because of your craving.

6. Bhaya

You see the dangers of the 5-Aggregates. In the simile of the house, you see the bank of the river disappearing with the consequent crumbling of the house.

You are in the swim of samsāra. You see decay, old age, death continually harassing you.

The cause of all this is craving that makes the 5-Grasping Aggregates to arise. Because you did not know the cause, which is craving, you are experiencing suffering all the time. You see danger in the arising of the 5-Aggregates.

7. A-dhi-nava

Means the faults or troublesome effects of the 5-Aggregates. You see the bad results. Suppose a person who is addicted to narcotics is continually asking for money and causes trouble. You see the trouble caused.

Say a man goes to a forest full of fearful things, like snakes and tigers, etc. You are fearful. Similarly the causes of the arising of the 5-Aggregates make you fearful. You fear sankhārā, the arising of the 5-Aggregates. They are full of lobha, dosa and moha. They are the cause of decay, old age and death.

8. Nibhida

You see the bad points of the 5-Aggregates. You see the defects, and you get fed up with sankhara. All is dukkha, suffering.

When you have a bad wife, you will hate her and also disgust will arise, etc. You decide that you must divorce her.

9. Muncitu Kamyata

You want to get out of the clutches of the 5-Aggregates. You want release from them.

10. Pati-sankha-nupassanā-ñāna, or Pati-sankha, for short.

You want your release and you must act. You work it out in detail.

There are 40 kinds in the 3 characteristics of

Anicca	10
Dukkha	25
Anatta	5
Total	40

As there are 5-Aggregates, this makes 200 Insights in all.

11. Sankharuppekha

The Aggregates arise by themselves and they cease by themselves. They arise with their own causes. You are now indifferent to everything. You are no longer affected by the good and bad in this world.

Whilst meditating, the sankharas, the 5-Aggregates disappear.

This feeling of indifference (uppekkha) is fostered by the balance of the mind or equanimity (tatra majjhatata).

12. Anuloma

When the Insight of Sankharuppekha matures, it changes itself into the insight of adaptation (anuloma-nana).

We are now nearing Magga. Out of Anicca, Dukkha, Anatta, one becomes predominant, whichever is fitting in the circumstances, but always pertaining to Magga.

Your wisdom becomes very alert, very strong, very quick.

13. Gotrabhu

You have finished with meditation on the 5-Aggregates. Change-of-lineage knowledge arises taking Nirvana as object.

It is the knowledge that sees the freedom from cause and effect.

It sees Nirvana, but not yet the 4-Noble Truths simultaneously.

14. Magga

This is the moment you have been striving for. In a flash of Magga Wisdom, you comprehend the 4-Noble Truths simultaneously.

15. Phala

Know that Magga has been achieved.

You are now a **Sottapanna**, a Stream-Entrant. You have overcome the first 3 Fetters, which are, belief in a permanent personality, clinging to rules and rituals, and doubt (scepticism).

You have 7 more Fetters to overcome. But you can rest on your oars, knowing there are only 7 more existences for you at a maximum, and you cannot be born in the lower planes.

16. Pacca-vekkhana

This is like the after-taste. You meditate on **Magga** and **Phala** and also on Nirvana.

When you reach the stage of sotāpanna, you know that 3 kilesas have been eliminated. You know that 7 more are remaining. You meditate on the remaining kilesas not yet eliminated.

As a sotāpanna, you have the added experience and wisdom that will make it easier to become a **Sakadāgāmi** and an **Anāgāmi**.

Every time you begin again at the **udaya-vaya-nana**. You meditate again on the 5-Aggregates, but with higher and better Insight.

But when you come to the stage that had previously been Gotrabhu, it becomes vodāna. Thereafter the sequence is anuloma, then vodāna, then magga and phala of sakadāgāmi.

The next time it is of an anāgāmi. And lastly you become an Arahat. You have reached your Goal.

Book II
Concentration

Introduction

This book deals with Concentration.

The Concentration is of the kind indulged in by the future-Buddha for the 6 years between his Renunciation and his final Enlightenment under the Bodhi Tree.

He achieved all the psychic powers that were attainable by concentration, including the 10 miraculous powers, and the super-normal knowledge like the Divine Eye and the Divine Ear, and recollecting the previous existences and the passing away and rebirth of beings, and also the 4 Formless States of the Sphere of Infinite Space, and the Sphere of Infinite Consciousness, and the Sphere of Nothingness and the Sphere of Neither-Perception nor Non-Perception. But he was satisfied that all these psychic powers solved the problem of Birth and Death, for the solution of which he had renounced his kingdom.

He was doing ordinary mundane concentration, and it was only when his mind switched on to meditation on ultimates that he finally achieved Enlightenment under the Bodhi Tree.

We must fathom our motives for doing either Concentration or Meditation. Concentration will produce the following psychic powers, and more:

> Clairvoyance;
> Clairaudience;
> Levitation of your body off the ground;
> Seeing the auras of others;
> Walking on water;

Concentration

>   Flying through the air;
>   Experiencing Joy and Bliss and Rapture,
>   which are beyond the ken of ordinary mortals;
>   Attaining the ecstatic state of mental tranquility;
>   Attaining the power of the Celestial Ear, by which you hear Sounds, both human and divine, both far and near;
>   Attaining the power of the Celestial Eye, by which you see material things and places regardless of distance, and by which you penetrate into the minds of others and read the nature of their thoughts;
>   Attaining the power of recalling your previous existences and the existences of others;
>   Attaining the powers of seeing beings pass away and their rebirth.

Meditation is meant for the person who is fed up with the cycle of **Samsāra**, being reborn again and again for millenniums and aeons, once as a man, next as a **deva** or an animal, and maybe for some time in hell or the upper reaches of the highest heavens. He is fed up with it all and does **Vipassanā** (Insight) Meditation towards achieving Freedom from Rebirth. At least, if he becomes a **Sotapanna**, he can rest on his oars, knowing that he cannot be born again in the realms of woe, including hell, and he has a maximum of only 7 existences before reaching Nirvana, the **Summum Bonum**.

Vipassanā Meditation is on ultimates and the three characteristics of existence, namely,

>   **Anicca**   (Impermanence),
>   **Dukkha** (Sorrow or Misery),
>   **Anatta**   (No Soul, No Self and No Control)

and will finally lead to **Magga** Wisdom and to **Nirvana**.

Buddhism is the only religion that promises its **Summum Bonum** in this existence.

So you have your choice as to what you want to do. This book will show you how. The psychic powers achieved by

Concentration are no mean thing, and the achieving of even some of these will take a life-time, and the fact that you are still an ordinary human being indicates that you are not yet freed.

There are a few expressions that we have to grapple with, namely, Mundane, Supra-mundane, Super-Normal, Super-Conscious, Transcendental and **Lokuttara**.

The question is whether the expression, 'Transcendental Concentration' is a contradiction in terms. All concentration is mundane, within the 31 planes of existence. Then the word 'super-mundane', which occurs in connection with Meditation, has been reserved for **Lokuttara**, where Nirvana is the object, as in the Noble 8-fold Path.

In which case, where does the word, 'Trancendental' come in? It is a question of translation. If the **Jhana** factors of Applied Thought (vitākka), Sustained Thought (vicarā), Joy (pīti), Bliss (**Sukha**) and one-pointedness (ekaggatā) are all transcended in turn to arrive at a higher stage of **Jhana**, it should not be wrong to call them Transcendental Minds.

Book I deals with Abhidhamma and Book II with Concentration. There is necessarily duplication of material in Book I and Book II, each book being sufficient unto itself, so that there is no need to read Book I if you confine yourself to Concentration.

Chapter 1

Your Mind

Transcendental Concentration is where the subject and the object meet and are fused as one. There is always a subject and an object, and they never meet except in Transcendental Concentration; they do not meet even in Transcendental Meditation.

There are 2 kinds of Mind Development and they are called:
1. Concentration or **Samatha Bhāvanā**, and
2. Meditation or **Vipassanā Bhāvanā**.

1. **Samatha** means calm; it leads to calm and tranquility and serenity. No previous knowledge of any Doctrine is necessary. You concentrate your Mind and you get the Psychic Powers.
2. **Vipassanā** leads to Insight Wisdom, and eventually to Nirvana, which is Peace.

The powers and capacities of the Human Mind are really wonderful and have been the subject of much wonder and speculation through the ages.

The source of these powers and capacities is in humans themselves and they can be attained by the Buddhist Methods of mental training.

We have to go about it in the right way, and you have to try hard enough. It is not so very difficult but it is not easy either.

The **Samatha** Method of Mental Training is based on Concentration. It requires just average intelligence. There is no need for a college education or even a high-school education. Concentration is a wonderful technique for inducing calm that will help you to face the tensions and pressures of everyday life.

Concentration may be called Relaxation, and **per se** will produce calmness of mind and body.

The main idea is to shut out external thoughts.

After a while, concentration becomes very pleasurable; you should cultivate a desire to concentrate. In due course it will be your ruling passion, your heart's delight, and you will be at it every spare moment, but do not let it interfere with your daily chores, your daily work.

But just wishing for results will lead you nowhere. You must not have your wishbone where your backbone ought to be.

There are many intensities of concentration ranging from the Preliminary or lowest stage to the highest or Perfect Stage, which is attained after much practice.

It is not difficult to achieve the Preliminary Stage of concentration. When you are reading a book and forget about the external world, you are exhibiting concentration of mind. When you go to a play and your mind is engrossed in the story, you are exhibiting concentration of mind. When you go to the movies and you suddenly lose awareness of the signs which say 'Exit' on the right or left of the screen, you are exhibiting concentration of mind. So you see that the possibility of concentration of mind is not beyond you.

Mind is popularly defined, for example, in the Chamber's Dictionary, as that which thinks, knows, feels and wills.

For our purpose, Mind can be defined as that which is conscious of an object and consciousness can be defined as the relation between subject and object.

Consciousness is subjective, but it can only arise when attention is present.

Concentration

Along with every consciousness arise certain mental constituents, otherwise called mental factors, or mental concomitants, mental adjuncts. Examples are: Love, Hate, Greed, Anger, Worry, etc.

Mind consists of consciousness plus a few mental factors. These mental factors total 52, and there are many combinations of these mental factors in each unit of consciousness.

1. Say, you see a girl. Visual consciousness has arisen. You have a reaction on seeing the girl. Certain mental factors have arisen; they could be good or bad. She may be a good girl or a bad girl. You may have prejudice against this girl or you may have a bias in her favour. You may have just heard something against her. There are so many possibilities for the mental reactions to arise.
2. You hear something. Aural consciousness has arisen. Once again, certain reactions arise, good or bad.
3. You taste something. Taste consciousness has arisen. There are so many possibilities for reaction to arise.
4. You smell something. Olfactory consciousness has arisen. Once again certain reactions arise, depending on whether you like or hate the smell.
5. You touch something. Tactile consciousness has arisen, and there are so many possible reactions to arise.
6. You think of something. Ideational consciousness has arisen, but it is not based on the 5 senses.

Once again, there are certain mental reactions.

Only one consciousness can arise at a time, namely, only one Mind can arise at a time.

One consciousness disappears before the next consciousness arises.

When there are so many competing outside objects, the stimulus that claims attention at the moment will produce the corresponding Mind.

The Mind works very fast. It is said that it takes about a billionth of a second for the Mind to arise, and it immediately disappears.

It is the Mind, and Mind alone, that is aware of, or knows, an object.

When anything is known, there are 2 things involved, namely, the Mind which knows, and the object which is the thing known.

The important thing is the Mind, for, without the Mind, the object cannot be known.

However, the Mind, instead of pointing to itself, has the habit practically of pointing to the object.

Take the case of a person looking up at something in the sky. Another person comes along and invariably, instead of looking at the first person, looks at the thing in the sky. Similarly a third person and so on.

The Mind is inclined towards the object. It is true that the Mind could look at itself, as it were, instead of inclining towards the object.

But can the Mind look at itself? When the Mind functions, it disappears immediately. One has to recall the Mind that has just disappeared and it becomes the object.

So the Mind cannot look at itself at the moment that it functions. Only after the first Mind has disappeared can we recall the first Mind.

The Human Personality or Ego consists of:

    1. Body, and
    2. Mind.

The Body and Mind is similar to the combination of a Blind Man and a Cripple. The Blind Man cannot see and the Cripple cannot walk. They join forces, and the Cripple is put on the shoulders of the Blind Man, and together they function. The Cripple can see and directs the Blind Man to go left and right, and the Blind Man obeys.

It is the Mind that wants, say, to drink and it is the Body that drinks. It is the Mind that wants to eat, and it is the Body that eats.

In every matter, it is the Mind that directs and the Body obeys.

All verbal and physical actions are motivated by the subjective Mind.

It is well known that old people cannot hear certain sounds that are audible to younger people. It does not mean, however, that these sounds do not exist.

Similarly, there are sound waves that are inaudible to humans. Moreover, if the Mind is abosrbed in something else and attention is not paid to these sounds, the Mind does not hear these sounds.

In these cases, the sounds do not exist for the Mind.

Only when the subjective Mind takes these sounds as objects can they be heard by a person and they exist for the Mind.

Similarly, things exist in the world but they are not known to the Mind, so long as they are not objects of the Mind.

However, the Mind cannot take everything as object at one and the same time. The Mind can take as an object one thing at any one time, and the rest of the world is non-existent so far as the Mind is concerned.

The Minds that have already disappeared are no more existent to the Mind, and the Minds as yet unborn are still non-existent. The Mind exists at the present moment only.

Chapter 2

Consciousness

Consciousnesses arise through the 5 sense-organs, or sense doors, as they are called, producing sense-consciousnesses in the brain. There is another door, called the Mind Door; when you day-dream or think of something not based on the 5 senses, Mind consciousness arises through the Mind Door.

There are 5 kinds of sense-consciousnesses. When a visual external stimulus makes contact with the eye organ, there arises an impression. At first it is an impression followed immediately by the eye-sense-consciousness.

Different external stimuli are competing for attention. An eye-sense stimulus may win, or it may be an ear-sense stimulus, or it may be a smell-sense stimulus, and so on. These impressions have to build up to a certain threshold to produce the sense-consciousness. Only when the impression is of sufficient strength will it be registered in the brain as a sense-consciousness. It is the attention that builds up the sense-consciousness and this is helped by interest. But whilst a sense-consciousness about something or other is about to fructify, distracting sense stimuli may rush in; large noises are the most distracting and push themselves into the brain to cause aural or hearing-sense-consciousness.

But as soon as a unit of consciousness arises, it disappears immediately, to be immediately followed by another unit of consciousness. The new unit of consciousness may be of the same character as the immediately past unit of consciousness; namely, a visual-sense-consciousness or it may be followed by another kind of consciousness, say, by an aural-sense-consciousness.

The Mind can be conscious of only one kind of consciousness at a time. With the arising of each unit of consciousness there also arise certain consciousness-accompaniments, otherwise known as thought constituents, or mental concomitants, or mental factors, such as love, hate, anger, fear, compassion, worry, etc., which accompany consciousness.

These thought-constituents arise in groups and some are mutually exclusive like love and hate. These groups form in many combinations, depending on whether the thoughts are selfish thoughts or unselfish thoughts, and so on.

A child's dominant instinct is the ego-instinct which makes it completely selfish. It has desires and wishes which cannot be fulfilled and are 'repressed'. They are the cause of much trouble in the form of nervous disorders, nightmares, hysteria, depression, and a host of other ailments. Also, certain 'complexes' are developed.

Your present character is the outcome of impressions formed in early childhood, and was moulded by your environment, and the attitude adopted by you towards your environment. Much of your behaviour, and even your thinking, is motivated by emotions and by repressed infantile desires.

At the moment of conception, your resultant karmic forces, in being translated into the new life, have already endowed the new embryonic cell with its genes, and its chromosomes, and DNA and RNA and its heredity. It is your karma that you should be born blind or deaf, etc.; all this has been fashioned at the moment of conception.

Every person from the time of conception has certain good and bad tendencies which have been implanted by the karma of past lives. It is up to him to change his future karma, to live with basic good conduct towards a more moral and spiritual life, or to go down the gutter leading an immoral life.

The new life is also endowed with good and bad animal instincts in varying proportions as a result of the karma of past lives. Again it is up to the person concerned to overcome his animal instincts and lead a rational life through concentration and meditation.

In Part I of the Book is mentioned that the functions of the human body are carried on automatically. No amount of conscious command can enable you, for example, to raise the rate of beating of your heart. But the least fear or anger will subconsciously make your pulse rate shoot up. Throughout the 24 hours of the day, whilst you are sleeping or you are awake, your body is receiving its orders; for example your heart and your stomach and your kidney and your liver, and the results are automatic. As your body grows, it builds up a wonderfully intricate system of nerves which also function automatically.

In the Universe, there are 3 Realms of existence:
1. The Realm of Sensuous Desire, ranging from the Purgatories through the Plane of Animals and the Human Plane to the Planes of Higher Beings within the Sense-World.
2. The Realm of Pure Form, where the Senses of Taste, Smell and Touch are eliminated, and only the mental, visual and aural senses remain. (The Mental Faculty is taken as a Sense.)
3. The Realm of Non-Form, where only the mental sense is present. (The Mental faculty is taken as a sense.)

In all, there are 89 consciousnesses:

1. Sensuous Realm ... 54 consciousnesses
2. Pure Form ... 15 consciousnesses
3. Non-Form ... 12 consciousnesses

        Total: 81

4. Supra-Mundane ... 8 consciousnesses

    Grand Total: 89

Chapter 3

The Superconscious Mind

The expression, "The Super-Conscious Mind" is used because many Buddhists will say that the term "Transcendental Concentration" is a contradiction in terms in that there is no Transcendental Mind in concentration but only in **Vipassanā** Meditation, and that is when you are nearing **Magga** Wisdom.

Yet, as you are transcending the different **Jhāna** factors of Applied Thought, Sustained Thought, etc., in **Jhāna** Concentration, as will be explained later, it should not be wrong to use the expression, "Transcendental Concentration".

The Superconscious Mind is mostly latent till called upon to function.

In the system of **Jhāna** training, it is called upon for the first time to function when your Mind achieves the first Jhāna with the elimination of the Five Hindrances simultaneously, as explained later. These 5 Hindrances are: Craving or Lust for Sensuous Desires, Ill-will, Sloth and Torpor, Restlessness and Worry and Skeptical Doubt.

There are many different forms of Concentration, but it is not every form of concentration that will induce **Jhāna**. For example, it is no use concentrating on a picture of a horse, for it will not induce **Jhāna**.

But if you concentrate on a picture of your brother, it will give you somewhat good concentration, but it will be difficult to eliminate all the 5 Hindrances simultaneously.

If you are going to concentrate on a picture of your sweetheart, you will not be able to surmount the first of the 5 Hindrances, which is Craving or Lust for Sensuous Desires.

When you have transcended the Realm of Sensuous Desires, you proceed thereafter to the Second Jhāna, where you will have to transcend Applied Thought and Sustained Thought.

As you proceed to the third Jhāna, you transcend Joy, as explained later.

As you proceed to the 4th Jhāna, you transcend Bliss, as explained later.

If you die whilst you are concentrating in the 1st Jhāna, as you have transcended the Realm of Sensuous Desires, you will be born in the Realm of Pure Form.

From the 1st Jhāna onwards through the Second and Third and Fourth Jhāna, you will be born as beings of radiant light, beings of boundless aura, beings of infinite radiance, and beings of the purity.

In the Realm of non-Form, where only the mental faculty is present, we have beings corresponding to the 4 stages of Non-Form Consciousness.

You may wish to achieve Transcendental Concentration in the Realm of Non-Form. Here you concentrate on formless objects, and the procedure is to transcend one stage before the next stage is achieved.

But after the 4th Jhāna, without going to the Realm of Non-Form, there are many supernormal powers in the Realm of Pure Form that can be attained.

There is the super-normal power of the Celestial Ear, which hears sounds, both human and divine, whether far or near. It is achieved by systematic practice after attaining the 4th Jhāna. You have to develop the capacity step by step so that you hear sounds at a great distance by means of Jhāna Concentration.

There is the super-normal power of the Celestial Eye by which you see material things and places from afar regardless of the distance and you can penetrate others' minds and read the nature of their thoughts.

Then there is the super-normal knowledge of the rebirth of beings. Here you develop the medium of light to such an extent that even night appears as day and makes the mind radiant. Then you can see beings passing away and beings born in happy or miserable circumstances according to their former deeds, good or bad.

Then there is the super-normal knowledge of recollecting your previous existences. After the 4th Jhāna, you should develop the faculty of memory, first recollecting the events of present life from the present moment up to the moment of birth and tracing its relation to your previous birth. You continue your concentration so that you can recollect as many former births as possible.

Then there are the 4 Arūpa Jhānas, namely,

1. the conception of the infinity of space,
2. the conception of the infinite consciousnesses,
3. the conception of nothingness,
4. the conception of neither-perception nor non-perception.

The above are mentioned, but it is doubtful whether you will go in for these 4 Arūpa Jhānas.

Chapter 4

Preliminary Concentration Exercises

Concentration means one-pointedness of Mind upon a single object. It is the narrowing of the field of attention.

It is said that Einstein scarcely ever needed pencil and paper in the first instance when solving mathematical problems. His concentration was so good that he could work out his problems in his head and only later would he commit them to paper.

It takes many many hours spread over days and months and maybe years to develop one-pointed concentration. You should exercise your will-power and do your concentration exercises at every available opportunity. If you are really serious, you should spend an hour or more non-stop every day on concentration, in addition to snatches of concentration at all available times of the day. It will pay dividends. After you have achieved one-pointed concentration, nothing will hold you back. You will want to spend more and more time on it.

You can concentrate for a few minutes at a time in any position or posture and in any place, but the best place for longer periods of concentration is in the quietness of your own room.

Concentration

Sit upright on a chair and place your arms comfortably on the arm rests. Keep your two feet on the ground; you can keep them crossed if you prefer. Or your feet can be kept dangling in the air if the chair is high. Keep the body erect. Try different chairs to find out the one you like best.

For long periods of concentration it is better to sit cross-legged in the "Turkish fashion". Sit down on a divan or on the floor with your legs stretched out. Bend your left leg at the knee and place it under the right thigh. Then bend the right leg at the knee and place it under the left leg. The position of the two legs may be reversed. If you are very uncomfortable at the start, sit on a low stool or a book or something, 2 or 3 or more inches high.

When sitting cross-legged in the Turkish Fashion with one shin over the other, there may in due course arise some aches and pains where they touch or overlap. A better cross-legged position is where the two shins do not touch at all; but it is difficult at first. When on the floor bend your left leg as usual bringing your left heel towards your body. Manoeuvre the right leg so that your bended right leg does not touch the bended left leg. This is easy if the junction of the thigh and the shin lies flat on the floor. Actually, if at first this junction is higher than the floor by a few inches, after some months of trying out this posture, one day the junction will lie flat on the floor. At the same time the junction made by your right leg will also lie flat on the floor. The position of the two legs may be reversed.

If you are uncomfortable at the start, you can sit on a book or a low stool some inches high.

Now you can concentrate for hours and hours without cramps and aches due to the touching of the shins.

The cross-legged posture per se has some calming effects on the body. After some time your pulse-rate will be reduced by as much as 5 to 10 beats, and the respiratory rate will come down to about 14 or 15 times a minute from the usual 18 or 19 or 20. To those very advanced in concentration, the respiratory rate has been known to come down to as little as 5 or 6 a minute.

It is important to keep the body erect. The hands can be placed anywhere where you find it comfortable.

Concentration Exercise No. 1

Take up your concentration posture. Breathe naturally, namely, do not force your breathing. Let your Sub-conscious do the breathing for you.

Now, just be aware of your in-breaths and out-breaths. Or in the alternative be aware of the in-breath striking the tip of your nose or striking any part of your upper lip (wherever it does strike).

Let there be no conceptual thought at all. Do not think of the past, nor of the future. Just live in the present, aware of the in-breaths and out-breaths.

It is possible that in course of time, the tip of your nose will seem to become a bit hard. You will feel a sensation of hardness at the tip of your nose. You can then concentrate on this sensation of hardness.

Concentration Exercise No. 2

When you are occupied in any activity, viz., reading, writing, talking, the idea is to maintain in your marginal zone of consciousness the awareness of the hardness of the tip of your nose. Your main activity will occupy the focal zone of consciousness but at the same time you must be aware, as mentioned above, in your marginal zone of consciousness.

When you are very much in love, are you not aware of your all-pervading love, though you are occupied with this or that chore, with this activity and that? Your love-awareness is in your marginal zone of consciousness. When you do your concentration exercises, you are concentrating by being aware of your in-breaths and out-breaths in the focal zone of consciousness. In course of time, you will achieve one-pointed concentration for half a minute, then for a minute, then for 5 minutes, then for much longer periods, when you are not aware of anything in your marginal zone of consciousness.

Concentration Exercise No. 3

Do one or both of these two arithmetical exercises. Close your eyes and rest them by visualising black.

NOW ADD AS FOLLOWS:—

$$
\begin{align*}
3 + 3 &= 6 \\
6 + 6 &= 12 \\
12 + 12 &= 24 \\
24 + 24 &= 48 \\
48 + 48 &= 96 \\
96 + 96 &= 192 \\
192 + 192 &= 384 \\
384 + 384 &= 768 \\
768 + 768 &= 1536
\end{align*}
$$

and so on.

THE SECOND EXERCISE IS TO ADD:—

$$
\begin{align*}
2 + 2 &= 4 \\
4 + 4 &= 8 \\
8 + 8 &= 16 \\
16 + 16 &= 32 \\
32 + 32 &= 64 \\
64 + 64 &= 128 \\
128 + 128 &= 256 \\
256 + 256 &= 512 \\
512 + 512 &= 1024 \\
1024 + 1024 &= 2048
\end{align*}
$$

and so on.

You can use your initiative and perform some more arithmetical exercises. For example:

$$7 + 7 = 14$$ and so on.

Concentration Exercise No. 4

Concentrate on something external to you. Look at a picture or a statue for some seconds and then visualise it in your mind's eye. Preferably you may wish to visualise a religious picture or statue. Look at the picture or statue again and again and visualise it; keep it up for minutes and minutes.

When you achieve deep concentration by losing consciousness of everything around you for minutes on end, you are making progress.

Concentration Exercise No. 5

In this Concentration Exercise you are required to do some forced chest breathing. Breathe fast, in and out. You can adopt long breaths or medium breaths or little breaths. In and out. But the breathing should be rhythmic, namely, the in-breaths should have the same timing. The frequency of respirations per minute may be anything from 100 to 150 or more.

You will find for yourself what is a good frequency of respiration for you. As your body will naturally be shaking because of your forced breathing, this Exercise is not feasible or pleasant when you are in a lying position. The best is the cross-legged position with your body erect, but it can be done when you are sitting in a chair.

People will notice your forced breathing and the shaking of your body and thus it should be done in the privacy of your room.

Carry on for minutes and minutes. The carbonic acid from your blood stream will gradually be reduced causing a gradual increase in alkalinity. If you breathe very hard for a very long time, you may feel a little dizzy, but there is nothing to worry about; you should stop and resume normal breathing for the present.

After starting your forced breathing, concentrate on the impact that your in-breaths and out-breaths make at the entrance of the nose or the upper lip. Be aware of the sensation of impact. Let there be no conceptional thinking, no thinking of the past and no thinking of the future. Just concentrate on the present, namely, be aware of the sensation of impact.

Every time your mind wanders, bring it back with an added burst of breathing. This method of breathing facilitates concentration.

Try the gimmick of short breaths, namely, short in-breaths and short out-breaths, so that the sensation of impact is continuous. For example, a cine-film consists of separate pictures but when projected on the screen at a certain minimum number of pictures per second, the persistence of vision makes you see animated scenes. Similarly, let there be a persistence of the sensation of impact making it a continuous sensation. You focus your mind on this continuous sensation.

Whatever may be your technique of forced breathing, your concentration should become better and better till you achieve one-pointed concentration, at first for half a minute, then a full minute, then for 5 minutes and then for more.

After some time of forced breathing, you consciously change over to calm rhythmic breathing, and then later you are no more aware of your breathing and are just concentrating on the in-breaths and out-breaths on the upper-lip, or wherever the impact is.

The period of forced breathing should become less and less as the weeks roll by, and you can move over more quickly into calm rhythmic breathing. But every time your mind wanders, bring it back with an effort of will with the help of a few bursts of forced breathing.

This forced breathing by itself will make you warm physically. You can keep yourself warm by this method. In warmer climates you will begin to perspire and sweat, and you should be careful not to catch a cold with your clothes all wet.

This forced breathing has therapeutic value. You will find that your phlegm is thrown up and you should have a handkerchief or something ready to catch the phlegm. Those with respiratory ailments should try this method from a healing point of view. But more about this is in a later chapter.

Concentration Exercise No. 6

In this Exercise you concentrate on sounds external to you. You can close your eyes but it is not an imperative. Or you can perform the Exercise sometimes with your eyes closed and sometimes with your eyes open.

Concentrate on sounds near to you, then on sounds far from you. It is a very interesting Exercise which you can perform at any place and at any time. Concentrate for minutes on end. Remember that it is a real Exercise and not just a pastime.

You will be surprised after a few weeks how acute your sense of hearing has become and it will have been worthwhile.

Concentration Exercise No. 7

In this Exercise you are to concentrate on smells external to you. It is a matter of choice whether you close your eyes or not, or you may want to close your eyes sometimes and open them sometimes.

Concentrate on smells near to you and on smells far from you. You can do this Exercise wherever you are and at anytime at your convenience. Really concentrate for minutes and minutes, and do not treat it just as a pastime.

After a few weeks your sense of smell will have become more acute and it may be of value to you sometime or other.

Chapter 5

Buddhist Method of Mental Culture

The future Buddha renounced his kingdom at the age of 29 and studied under the best Teachers of the day. He did Concentration under Hermit Alara and Hermit Ramapatta.

Later he took to ascetic practices along with his 5 Companions, known as the 5 Vaggi.

He achieved all the psychic powers that could be obtained. He also attained to the 4 **Arūpa** or Formless states of

1. the conception of the infinity of space;
2. the conception of infinite consciousness;
3. the conception of nothingness;
4. the conception of neither-perception nor non-perception.

But he was not satisfied in that what he had achieved did not solve the problem of birth and death. He became very emaciated and one day he fell down in a swoon.

He realised that he was not on the right track by just concentrating his mind. He took to food again.

It was on the full-moon day of May that he meditated under the Bodhi Tree in present day Buddha-Gaya. He changed from **Samādhi** Concentration to **Vipassanā** Meditation and became Enlightened, and was known later as Gautama Buddha.

Mental Culture

The method he used for his Concentration and Meditation, and by which he achieved Enlightenment, was by being mindful of His In-Breaths and Out-Breaths, called Ānā-Pāna. (Pronounced Ar-nar-par-na.)

However, when he developed the methods of Mental Development for his Disciples, he formulated 40 **kammathāna** subjects as objects of concentration and meditation. They are as follows:

1. The 10 **Kasinas,** which are the 10 devices
2. The 10 **Asubhas,** being concentration on corpses
3. The 10 **Anussatis,** being the 10 Recollections
4. The 4 **Brahma-Vihāras**
5. The 4 **Arūpas,** being the Sphere of Space, the Sphere of consciousness, the Sphere of Nothingness, and the Sphere of Neither-Perception nor Non-Perception.
6. The contemplation of the Loathsomeness of Food
7. Analysis of the 4 Physical Elements

Ana-Pana Concentration and Meditation comes under No. 3 above.

These 40 **Kammathāna** subjects have been described in great detail in the Scriptures. Except for 4 or 5 of them, it is doubtful whether they will be used by readers of this book.

1) The 10 **Kasinas,** or Devices are:
    1. Earth Device
    2. Water Device
    3. Fire Device
    4. Air or Wind Device
    5. The Blue Device
    6. The Yellow Device
    7. The Red Device
    8. The White Device
    9. Space Device
    10. Consciousness Device

2) The 10 **Asubhas** are concentrations on corpses in their different stages of decomposition.

3) The 10 **Anussatis** or Recollections are:
   1. Recollection of the Buddha
   2. Recollection of the Dhamma
   3. Recollection of the Sangha
   4. Recollection of Virtue
   5. Recollection of Charity
   6. Recollection of the Devas
   7. Mindfulness of Death
   8. Mindfulness of the Physical Body
   9. Mindfulness of Breathing (**Ana-Pana**)
   10. Recollection of Calmness

4) The **Brahma-Viharas** of
   a) Loving Kindness (**Metta**)
   b) Compassion (**Karunā**)
   c) Sympathy (**Mudita**)
   d) Equanimity (**Uppekkha**)

Each Concentration has its usefulness in the scheme of Buddhist Mental Culture.

There is a Chapter on the Earth Device, under the title, 'Walking on Water'.

There are 2 Chapters on Mindfulness of Breathing (**Ana-Pana** and **Jhāna** Concentration.)

There is a Chapter on Loving-Kindness or **Metta**.

Chapter 6

Āna-Pāna, or Mindfulness of Breathing

Mindfulness of Breathing, called **Ana-Pana** (Pronounced Arnar-Parna), is described on p. 285 of the Path of Purification (**Visuddhi-Magga**), translated by Bikkhu Nanamoli. It runs as follows:

It has been described by the Blessed One as having sixteen bases thus: 'And how developed, bhikkhus, how practised much, is concentration through mindfulness of breathing both peaceful and sublime, an unadulterated blissful abiding, banishing at once and stilling evil unprofitable thoughts as soon as they arise?

'Here, bhikkhus, a bhikkhu, gone to the forest or to the root of a tree or to an empty place, sits down; having folded his legs crosswise, set his body erect, established mindfulness in front of him, ever mindful he breathes in, mindful he breathes out.

(i) Breathing in long, he knows "I breathe in long"; or breathing out long, he knows "I breathe out long".

(ii) Breathing in short, he knows "I breathe in short"; or breathing out short, he knows "I breathe out short".

(iii) He trains thus "I shall breathe in experiencing the whole body", he trains thus "I shall breathe out experiencing the whole body".

(iv) He trains thus "I shall breathe in tranquillizing the bodily formation"; he trains thus "I shall breathe out tranquillizing the bodily formation".

(v) He trains thus "I shall breathe in experiencing happiness"; he trains thus "I shall breathe out experiencing happiness".

(vi) He trains thus "I shall breathe in experiencing bliss"; he trains thus "I shall breathe out experiencing bliss".

(vii) He trains thus "I shall breathe in experiencing the mental formation"; he trains thus "I shall breathe out experiencing the mental formation".

(viii) He trains thus "I shall breathe in tranquillizing the mental formation"; he trains thus "I shall breathe out tranquillizing the mental formation".

(ix) He trains thus "I shall breathe in experiencing the (manner of) consciousness"; he trains thus "I shall breathe out experiencing the (manner of) consciousness".

(x) He trains thus "I shall breathe in gladdening the (manner of) consciousness"; he trains thus "I shall breathe out gladdening the (manner of) consciousness".

(xi) He trains thus "I shall breathe in concentrating the (manner of) consciousness"; he trains thus "I shall breathe out concentrating the (manner of) consciousness".

(xii) He trains thus "I shall breathe in liberating the (manner of) consciousness"; he trains thus "I shall breathe out liberating the (manner of) consciousness".

(xiii) He trains thus "I shall breathe in contemplating impermanence"; he trains thus "I shall breathe out contemplating impermanence".

(xiv) He trains thus "I shall breathe in contemplating fading away"; he trains thus "I shall breathe out contemplating fading away".
(xv) He trains thus "I shall breathe in contemplating cessation"; he trains thus "I shall breathe out contemplating cessation".
(xvi) He trains thus "I shall breathe in contemplating relinquishment"; he trains thus "I shall breathe out contemplating relinquishment".

This Mindfulness, unlike other **kammathanā** subjects, is for both **Samatha** and **Vipassanā**, and goes from **Samatha** to **Vipassanā**. However, it is too very difficult, as the language is very involved.

The best thing is to follow the **Jhāna** arisings as described in Chapter 14 and to follow the **Vipassanā** Meditation as described in Chapter 7.

Regarding the subject of Concentration, we should be acquainted with the general terminology. It will help you to understand this book and other books.

The attempt made by the aspirant in fixing his mind on the object is called **Parikamma-Bhāvanā**. There are many kinds of objects and it is the first concentration on the object that is called **Parikamma Bhāvanā**. When the object, called the symbol, is thoroughly grasped by the Mind, and appears as if the aspirant sees it with the eyes open, he is said to have obtained the visualised image; it is a concept called **Uggaha-Nimitta**, which is the mental replica of the symbol.

The attempts made to make the visualised object clearer and brighter than the actual object as seen by the open eyes is called **Upacāra-Bhāvanā**. This brighter concept is called the **Pathibhaga-Nimitta**, which is the 'after-image'.

As soon as the 5 Hindrances are suppressed, **Upacāra-Samādhi** is obtained and is otherwise called Access or Proximate Samādhi. The Mind is not yet steady even at this stage. **Upacāra-Samādhi** is proximate to **Appanā-Samādhi**.

Concentration

Appanā-Samādhi is full-fledged concentration; the aspirant can stay in this stage for as long as he wants, for the 5 Hindrances have been eliminated. With the attainment of Appanā-Samādhi, he has attained the 1st Jhāna.

So the process runs as follows:

Parikamma-Upacara-Anuloma-Gotrabhu-Appana

The Mind-Consciousness now takes the **Patibhaga-Nimitta** and prepares it for the first stage of Jhāna.

In turn we get **Upacāra** (Access) and **Anuloma**, which is called Adaptation consciousness. Then comes **Gotrabhū**, where the thought-moment transcends the sensuous plane. The former lineage has been cut off and the Mind evolves the lineage of the Form Plane. This is immediately followed by **Appanā-Samādhi**, which is Ecstatic Concentration. This is First Jhāna, otherwise called **Rūpa-Jhāna**.

Chapter 7

Jhāna Concentration

The words **Samatha**, **Samādhi** and **Jhāna** are mostly used synonymously. They all mean Concentration.

Samadhi literally means "placing firmly together" (sam-a-dha). The word **Sammā-samādhi** is one of the mental factors of the Noble 8-fold Path and was used by the Buddha himself.

Jhāna corresponds to the Sanskrit 'dhyana', and is derived from the root 'Jhe' which means 'to think' or 'to meditate', namely, to think closely or meditate firmly upon a given object. **Jhāna** is both a system of mental training and a process of transforming the lower states of consciousness to higher levels.

In the Second Basket of the Scriptures, namely, the Suttas, there are 4 **Jhānas**, but in the Third Basket, the Abhidhamma, there are 5 **Jhānas**. They are practically the same; in the Suttas, the first 2 of the 5 mental factors have been coalesced.

The main idea of concentration is to fuse the subject and the object, and this is achieved at the higher levels of consciousness. At first, concentration is helped by the will.

There are two separate levels. At the bottom it is calm, whilst at the surface there is discursive thinking. The practice of concentration calms the surface.

The general idea is to transcend the Sensuous Realm bringing the Mind to the Realm of Pure Form, and then later to

121

Concentration

transcend the **Jhāna** Factors of Applied Thought, Sustained Thought, Joy and Bliss till one attains perfect one-pointedness of Mind and equanimity. The last is reached in the 4th **Jhana**.

Your decision to concentrate is the important step. It means that you have the desire and the will to get rid of your worries and your fears and your restlessness, as the case may be. The difficulty with most people is that they subconsciously enjoy being worried and being restless.

First **Jhāna**

Concentrate on your in-breaths and out-breaths at the tip of your nose. Whatever you may be doing or not doing, your sub-conscious carries on with your breathing, and it is a simple matter to concentrate on something which occurs automatically all the time.

Sit down quietly on a chair and concentrate on your in-breaths and out-breaths. The best place to concentrate on your in-breaths and out-breaths is at the nostrils, but you can try the alternative of concentrating on the rise and fall of your belly as you inhale and exhale.

If you have the time and the inclination, and you want to concentrate for more than half an hour, it is better to sit cross-legged in the "Turkish Fashion" on a divan or on the floor. Sit with your legs stretched out, and then bend your left leg at the knee and place it under the right thigh. Then bend the right leg at the knee and place it under the left leg. The position of the two legs may be reversed. If you are very uncomfortable at the start, sit on a low stool or a book or something, 2 or 3 or more inches high.

When sitting cross-legged in the Turkish fashion one shin is over the other, and in due course there may arise some aches and pains where they touch or overlap.

A better cross-legged position is when the two shins do not touch at all, but it is difficult at first. When on the floor bend your left leg as usual, bringing your left heel towards your body. Then manoeuvre the right leg so that your bended right leg does not touch your bended left leg. This is easy if the junction of the thigh and the shin lies flat on the floor. Actually, if at first this junction is higher than the floor by a few inches, after some months of trying out this posture, one day the junction will lie flat on the floor. At the same time the junction made by your right leg will also lie flat on the floor. The position of the two legs may be reversed.

You should be able to concentrate for hours and hours without cramps and aches, and this is possible by assuming a correct posture.

Concentrate on your breathing. Let your subconscious direct your breathing, and you are just to be aware in the first instance whether your in-breath is long or short, and whether your out-breath is long or short.

As an aid to concentration, you can count your breaths. 1. (one) for the first in-breath, and 2. (two) for the first out-breath, and 3. (three) for the next in-breath, and 4. (four) for the next out-breath, and so on up to 15 or so. You can repeat this for a number of times till you think that your mind has become somewhat calm.

Now you can concentrate on your in-breaths and out-breaths at your nostrils or the tip of your nose. Keep on concentrating for as long as you want, or for as long as you can.

It may be better for you to begin with short breaths — not very short, but more short than long. It takes some doing. It is more difficult than you think. Before you can get some sort of concentration, your mind has gone elsewhere, and you have to bring it back to where you started.

It is better to consider that there are two zones of consciousness or awareness, namely, the focal zone where your mind is in proper focus, and the marginal zone where you are aware of something somewhat in the background and where your awareness is a bit out of focus but you are aware of it all the same.

It is sometimes said that it is not correct to say that there are two zones of consciousness; the mind works so fast, in less than a billionth of a second, that there are really two different successive minds, but you think there is only one.

Concentration

Whatever it may be, try this exercise. When next you drive your car, be aware of whatever you are doing as you drive your car, but also in the marginal zone of awareness be aware of your breathing in and out. Do not think of anything else except your driving in the focal zone of your consciousness and of your breathing in and out in the marginal zone of your consciousness. You will be surprised how much more alert you are; you will have become a much better driver.

During the day when you are performing any task, perform the task with the focal zone of your consciousness, and at the same time be aware of your in-breaths and out-breaths in the marginal zone of your consciousness. You may have some difficulty at first but you will come to enjoy this concentration exercise as time goes by.

At first there are 3 thoughts, the first is the thought of the in-breath at the nose-door, the second is the thought of the out-breath, and the third is the contact at the nose-door. Later, these three thoughts are merged into one.

Even if you start with short breaths, the breathing eventually goes into long breaths.

After some time, the breathing apparently ceases. You cannot say whether you are breathing or not, the breathing is so refined and delicate.

You must make an effort to maintain rhythmical breathing.

First there is what is called "Preliminary Concentration".

The objective is the suppression of the 5 Hindrances which are impediments to good concentration, namely,

    1. Craving for sense-pleasures
    2. Ill-will
    3. Sloth and torpor
    4. Restlessness and worry; and
    5. Perplexity and skeptical doubt

They are defilements which are inimical to the clear Mind, and therefore must be suppressed; otherwise the Mind will not be concentrated.

They can only be suppressed at this stage and cannot yet be eliminated. It is only after achieving the First zone, and thereafter, that they are automatically eliminated.

When your concentration is getting better and better, and you have Basic Good Conduct, you will get your Sign.

This sign is different to different people. To some it is like a lotus, or a round jewel or pearl, to others like a column of smoke, the sun, the full-moon, starshine, a silver girdle-chain, a garland of flowers, a spreading cloud.

Once you get the Sign you must concentrate on it and leave aside the breaths and the "nose-door".

The sign must now be carefully guarded and fostered. It must be made to grow at will.

You must now be careful of the company you keep and not mix with persons who are not spiritually inclined.

You must be careful of the kind of talk you indulge in, for talk is the result of thoughts. You must avoid useless and aimless talk, as otherwise your induced image will disappear.

You must also take care of the food you eat to ensure that it is not unsuitable and cause you bodily trouble at this stage of your mental development.

You must also now try and see whether it is better for your concentration when you are sitting or lying down or standing or walking.

At this stage it is best to delimit the size of the induced image. It is no use having it too large. Enlarge the induced image to any size you want, but do not have it too big.

When the 5 Hindrances have been suppressed simultaneously, Ecstatic Concentration is obtained. This is the First Jhāna. This is when the Super-conscious Mind takes over.

With the First Jhāna, you have the Jhāna factors of Applied Thought, Sustained Thought, Deep Interest or Joy, Bliss and One-pointedness.

This complete absorption transcends the Realm of Sensuous Desire, and brings you to the Realm of Form.

You are now ready to proceed to the Second Jhāna.

Second Jhāna

The Second Jhāna is attained by transcending applied thought and sustained thought.

When you have attained the First Jhāna and obtained proficiency therein, you review your achievement.

You feel that your mind is not quite so calm, disturbed as it is by waves of Applied Thought and Sustained Thought. The latter are gross in nature and you are threatened by the 5 Hindrances.

At this stage you require personal confidence and great exaltation of mind.

As concentration proceeds, you will now experience joy which refreshes the mind and body.

There are many forms and intensities of joy, ranging from the joy that raises the hair of the body, to the joy that raises you off the ground, sometimes to the ceiling, to the joy that breaks over your body like waves on the sea-shore, to the joy which is all embracing and suffuses both body and mind.

With all this joy of excitement, your body will not be tired. You will feel light as you are refreshed.

You now make a big attempt to transcend Applied Thought and Sustained Thought, and you attain the second Jhāna.

Third Jhāna

Emerging from the second Jhāna, you review its factors with self-awareness and mindfulness. You are aware of its defects and that you are threatened by Applied Thought and Sustained Thought.

The joy you have experienced appears gross, whereas Bliss and Concentration make for peace of mind.

You must transcend Joy whilst remaining in equanimity of Jhāna, which is like indifference or disinterestedness. You are unaffected by pleasure or pain.

If you are not careful, the mind will return to Joy again.

You continue your concentration on the sign or after-image.

As soon as Joy is transcended, Bliss together with Concentration is achieved and you have attained to the third Jhāna. You are now blissful and even-minded.

Fourth Jhāna

You are still threatened by Bliss. You are therefore to transcend Bliss.

You keep concentrating as before. You become free from both pleasure or pain, either physical or mental. There is a difference in this world between physical and mental pain. Whatever may be your spiritual development, you will experience bodily pain till you die, but when you have attained to great spiritual development, there is no more the feeling of mental pain.

You now have a neutral feeling, of neither pleasure nor pain.

You now have the purest mindfulness through equanimity. There was a vestige of equanimity before in the previous stages of Jhāna, but now it is manifested to the full.

There is now perfect equilibrium of the mental states, which is the ultimate aim of Jhāna.

You are free from all kinds of mental disturbances. You are serene.

You have now achieved Perfect Concentration, with perfect stillness of both body and mind.

It is ecstatic concentration. You have achieved the fourth Jhāna.

At this stage you have achieved super-normal psychic powers of clairvoyance and clairaudience, and of seeing the auras of others.

Chapter 8
Walking on Water

Eastern philosophies state that the universe is composed of the primordial essences of Earth, Water, Fire and Air. They are also called fundamental elements. They are not material elements in the crude sense but are immaterial qualities and the concept is different from the Greek ones.

An atom is a unit of energy but can be made to materialise by combination with other atoms. Every manifestation of matter has the qualities of the fundamental elements of Earth, Water, Fire and Air in different combinations. These immaterial qualities can be made to materialise by the power of the Mind.

Of the many different concentration exercises on this and that, four important ones are on Earth, Water, Fire and Air.

The concentration on Earth gives you the power to walk on water and to stand on water, or to sit on water or to step on water by materialising earth.

The present chapter refers to concentration on Earth. Obtain or make a disc about eight to ten inches in diameter painted dull light pink or beige, or any very light colour. This disc is made of matter, of "Earth". The overall effect should not be bright or shining.

You must make a preliminary survey of why you want to do this concentration exercise. All concentration **per se** produces peace of mind and serenity and tranquility, but certain concentration exercises produce special effects. On the road to the production of the ultimate result, there are certain intermediate results which are themselves worthwhile obtaining.

Everybody is born with certain good and bad tendencies and one of the reasons for Transcendental Concentration is the suppression or elimination of the bad tendencies.

Certain desires arise through your contact with the outside world through your five senses. Many of these desires are selfish desires and one of the results of Transcendental Concentration is the overcoming of selfish and unwholesome desires.

Transcendental Concentration requires much sustained effort. You will have to be at it for weeks and weeks and months and months. You must have great eagerness to embark on this type of concentration, and all the time you must display sustained effort.

You have to look at the disc for minutes and minutes and maybe for hours. What posture of body will you adopt? Of the four postures of sitting, standing, walking and lying down, the last two are clearly unsuitable. Moreover, you cannot be standing for minutes and minutes and for hours. Therefore only the sitting posture is suitable.

You can sit comfortably on a chair, or you can sit cross-legged on a divan or on the floor. Sit about three or four or five feet away from the disc keeping it about the level of your eyes.

Before you begin your concentration exercise, calm down your body and your feelings and your emotions. Think of your body; think of the posture of your body, whether you are sitting or lying or standing, etc., and then calmly suggest to yourself that your body is at ease. Now think of your feelings; calm your feelings. Then think of your emotions; calm your emotions so that your mind is in a passive state.

Concentration

With half-open eyes concentrate looking at the disc. Look at it intently for a while as if you were looking at a beautiful picture.

Do not stare at it; blink your eyes naturally without being conscious of the blinking. Do not strain your eyes or your body. Look at it comfortably but with concentration. Then on closing your eyes see whether a visualised image appears in your mind's eye. If you lose it, try again and again. Keep it up for minutes and minutes till you see the visualised image clearly.

Keep on concentrating on the visualised image. The aim of concentration is to unify your mind with the object concentrated on. You must be able to maintain the visualised image in your mind when you walk away from your original position. If you lose it, go back to the disc and repeat the process all over again.

As you concentrate, you must completely forget the colour of the disc. The colour of the disc does not come into it at all. What is important is to know that you are making this Concentration Exercise on "Earth". You will have to remind yourself of it off and on by repeating the expression "Earth, Earth" at suitable intervals.

Before the visualised image appears in your mind, you may have to look at the disc a few hundred times or even a few thousand times, till you have the visualised image steady in your mind, whether your eyes be shut or open.

When you walk away from the disc, keep the visualised image in your mind wherever you go. If you lose the image, you must go back to the disc over and over again with sustained effort.

After you can keep the visualised image in your mind for an appreciable amount of time, there will arise in your mind what may be called the After-image. The disc will appear shining and bright like a looking glass and with no colour or shape.

You should delimit the size of the After-image. Enlarge it to any size you want, but do not have it too big.

You should be careful of the company you keep and the kind of talk you indulge in and take care of the food you eat.

You must see whether it is better for your concentration when you are sitting or lying down or standing or walking.

And now the Five Hindrances are suppressed, as mentioned previously in the Chapter on Jhāna Concentration on in-breaths and out-breaths.

When the 5 Hindrances are suppressed, you are no more in the Realm of Sensuous Desire, and you achieve the First Jhāna.

Thereafter, the procedure is similar up to the Fourth Jhāna, but you must remind yourself off and on that this Concentration is on "Earth".

After the 4th Jhāna, you will have the power of Walking on Water.

Chapter 9

Concentration on Loving-Kindness

There is enough hatred and prejudice and misunderstanding all over the world for us to want to surmount them.

We want goodwill and friendship, free from malice and anger, in thought and deed and word, to guide our life with our relatives and friends and our neighbours and the rest of the whole wide world.

This Chapter deals with concentration on Loving-kindness. Loving-kindness means "love without lust" or friendliness or spiritual love. It is the opposite of hatred or ill-will or anger, and this Concentration Exercise gets rid of anger and malice.

It is the habitual mental attitude of goodwill and friendship.

It is the opposite of hatred or ill-will or anger, and this concentration gets rid of malice and anger.

There are two ideas behind this Concentration Exercise. One is to suffuse the whole world with loving-kindness, and the other is to extend loving-kindness to particular human beings.

But in order to suffuse the whole world with loving-kindness, or to extend loving-kindness to particular human beings, it is necessary in the first instance to suffuse oneself with loving-kindness. Only then will you be able practically to extend loving-kindness to the whole world and to particular human beings.

So let us begin with that. One-self is the easiest person to suffuse with loving-kindness, for one-self is the dearest person to one-self.

Yet this part is a means to an end, as the end is to suffuse the whole world, and also particular beings, with loving-kindness.

Say to yourself: "I wish to be happy and free from misery, and so do all other persons. May I be free from ill-will and anxiety."

Then radiate loving-kindness on one-self. Then extend the loving-kindness to your Parents and to your Teachers.

Then extend loving-kindness to your dearest friend. You should avoid extending loving-kindness to your sweetheart, for it may turn to lust and not loving-kindness.

Then later to your enemy; this may be difficult at first, but you should persist in your attempt.

Then comes the second part. Say to yourself many times: "May all beings be happy and free from ill-will and anxiety and enmity."

Turn your loving-kindness on to the Northern portion of the world, and suffuse this portion of the world with loving-kindness.

Then turn your loving-kindness to the Eastern portion of the world, and suffuse this portion with your loving-kindness.

Then turn your loving-kindness to the Southern portion of the world, and suffuse this portion with your loving-kindness.

Then turn your loving-kindness to the Western portion of the world, and suffuse this portion with your loving-kindness.

Then turn to the regions above, and suffuse this portion with your loving-kindness.

Then turn to the regions below, and suffuse this portion with your loving-kindness.

Book III

Some Auto-Suggestions

Chapter 1

Breathing

Deep breathing is the very basis of all-round good health. Deep breathing should be a habit.

When we are asleep, the Subconscious Mind directs the breathing. Also when we are awake the Subconscious Mind directs the breathing except when we are consciously directing it, as when we are doing Breathing Exercises.

An average person breathes in and breathes out round about 19 times a minute. Deep breathing means that the frequency is 14 times a minute or lower.

There are two ways of breathing, namely, belly breathing where the diaphragm rises for the in-breath and falls for the out-breath, and chest breathing. The correct breathing for general purposes is belly breathing. When you have run a race and are winded and are gasping for breath, you do chest breathing. Your body requires oxygen quickly and this is obtained by chest breathing.

Deep breathing should be a life-long habit. Whether you are lying on a bed or sitting or standing or walking, you should do belly breathing. As you inhale, allow your diaphragm to rise up and your sides to fill out, and as you exhale there should be a gradual collapse of the diaphragm and of the sides.

Auto-Suggestions

You must not mix up in your mind the frequency of your breaths and the pulse rate, namely, the rate of beating of your heart. Conscious slow breathing for only a short while will not slow down your pulse rate immediately. Only prolonged conscious slow breathing, which will automatically be accompanied by a relaxation of your emotions, will reduce your pulse rate. The habit of deep breathing will reduce your pulse rate, which is very desirable.

Here are a few deep breathing Exercises:

General deep breathing

Inhale slowly, through the nose, mentally counting 1, 2, 3, 4, 5. Exhale through the nose; count the same 1, 2, 3, 4, 5. As a variation do not count when exhaling, and pay no heed whether you take a longer time than it takes to count 1, 2, 3, 4, 5 or a shorter time than 1, 2, 3, 4, 5.

Inhale and exhale for at least 20 times. If you have the time, breathe in and out for 30 times or more. You cannot overdo the Exercise. When you have finished your Exercise each day, your Subconscious will take over and carry on with your breathing.

You should do this Exercise many times a day, the more the merrier.

After you have fully breathed out through the nose, you will be surprised to find that you can still breathe out some more air through your mouth. There is no great merit in breathing out through the mouth, but you may want to play about with it, especially when you come to the stage of real deep breathing.

The next day, count up to 6 for the in-breaths and keep increasing every day up to 10. Later increase by one for every 2 days. Then every 3 days. You will know by now when you need not increase any further.

As a variation from gradual slow inhalation, try separate bouts of sniffing. If you are to count up to 5, take 5 sniffs instead. There is no advantage in sniffing as opposed to gradual inhalation, but it may help in your counting.

Breathing Before Sleep

When you are in bed just before going to sleep, deep breathing is a sleep-inducer. When breathing, count the same numbers 1, 2, 3, 4, 5 as you did in the morning and during the day. As you increase to 6 the next morning, increase likewise when in bed that night. When you are feeling drowsy, your Subconscious will take over and you will soon be asleep.

Walking and Jogging

When walking, take two in-breaths for the first two steps, left, right, and exhale for the next two steps, left, right. Then keep repeating. After some time, you will find that you can walk at a faster rate than before. Keep up the rhythm, even when talking to friends during your walk. When playing golf, you will find an added interest between your shots.

Jogging for a mile a day will keep you fit. It will improve your blood circulation, and good blood circulation is a sine qua non for good health. Breathe in and out as in walking, namely, breathe in for two consecutive steps, left, right, and breathe out for the next two consecutive steps, left, right. You should try the experiment of breathing in for every 4 steps and breathing out for every 4 steps. Later, when you cannot maintain the breathing for every 4 steps, breathe in for every 3 steps and breathe out for every 3 steps. You may have some difficulty at first in breathing in and breathing out for every 3 steps, but you can do it if you try. Then end up with breathing in and out for every 2 steps.

At the end of your jogging or running, when you are out of breath and gasping, you must do chest breathing and not belly breathing. If you are now stationary, breathe with your chest, in, out, in, out, quickly till your chest breathing can be slower and deeper. Carry on till you recover your breath and can change over to belly breathing. If you however choose to walk after a bit of jogging, breathe with your chest once for every step, namely, in with the left and out with the right. Or you may have to breathe in and out once for every step. There need be no fixed rule. Carry on till you have regained your breath and can change over to belly breathing.

Walking up Steps

When walking up steps, you should breathe as when walking. Breathe in for the first two steps and breathe out for the next two steps. You will be surprised how much easier it is to walk up steps when breathing correctly. When you are fit physically you can run up steps while breathing correctly and not lose your breath so easily.

Healing Breath

Say you are counting 5 for the in-breath. Now keep the air in your chest for double the number of counts; in this case, 10. Then exhale through your nose as quickly or as slowly as you want. You can try exhaling completely through your mouth, and this will help to fill your lungs in your next in-breath.

Repeat for 10 or 20 times more. This Exercise is good for those with respiratory ailments.

Chapter 2

Sleep and Insomnia

We are all brought up with the idea that both the body and the mind require some rest during the 24 hour-cycle period. Many doctors recommend 8 hours' sleep.

However, for those whose minds are over-activated for some reason or other, sleep does not come easily. The mental overactivity may be due to fear or worry or anxiety or even to excitement caused by extrema joy, mostly unexpected joy. Some keep awake for hours, tossing right and left in bed. The more they worry about their inability to sleep, the more awake they become. Eventually when their minds have become somewhat weary and deadened, they pass into sleep.

Actually 8 hours of sleep are not necessary every night. Many people have stayed awake for days without loss of efficiency in either mental or physical work. Insufficient sleep for one night does not impair one's efficiency in any way. Professional golfers have been known to be able to woo sleep for just a few hours and go on to play well the next day. What is worrisome is your worry that if you do not get a good night's rest you will suffer some inefficiency the next day. It has been proved over and over again that the mere fact of staying in bed with your eyes fully closed though tossing about from side to side for hours on end recuperates the body and also recuperates the mind to a very great extent.

When you really want to sleep, you must be able by a conscious effort to prepare your mind for sleep. After your mind has wandered here and there for minutes, and maybe for hours, on end, you must make a deliberate effort to go to sleep. From that moment of decision, it will not be difficult to fall off to sleep.

Make a big yawn by opening your mouth as wide as you can, and say to yourself a few hundred times, 'Want to sleep', 'Want to sleep'. This is on a par with the gimmick of 'counting sheep' followed by certain people.

The time is now ripe to make a suggestion to your subconscious that you are feeling sleepy, that you are feeling drowsy. Make your mind weary by the following rhythmic repetition:

> I am feeling
> drowsier and drowsier,

with the following kind of rhythm:

> Lar, la-lar,
> Larlar, la-lar.

Keep on and on, uttering the words mentally with the above rhythm. And you will find yourself dozing off.

Some people find that they want something longer than the above, and find the following more suitable:

> Moment by moment,
> And hour by hour,
> And I am feeling,
> Drowsier and drowsier,

with the rhythm somewhat as follows:

> Lar, la-lar,
> la-lar, la-lar,
> la-lar, la-lar,
> la-lar, la-lar.

You will soon be asleep. Keep it up, keep it up, till you are no more conscious.

In your own mind the abovementioned words may not suggest the above rhythm. Establish your own rhythm, your own lilt.

Possibly at some time before or during the rhythmic repetition, you wish to change the position of your body. Do so; turn over to your right or to your left and assume a comfortable sleeping posture. You will soon find out what posture is good for you, what posture you like. Keep up your rhythmic repetition, and you will soon be asleep.

Block conceptual thought, block verbal thinking, and when you mentally utter the rhythmic repetition with concentration, it will not be difficult to go off to sleep.

The above is for those not suffering from acute insomnia. If you suffer from insomnia, you will not be able to get yourself to the stage of making the suggestion to your subconscious, as stated above. You will have to be more drastic and begin by preparing your body for sleep.

After making your decision to go to sleep, you must prepare your body for sleep by relaxing. After your body has been relaxed, you prepare your emotions for sleep.

You are now in bed. The best position for a start is lying flat on your back with your face facing the ceiling, and your eyes closed. Let your hands be on either side of your body and your legs uncrossed and stretched straight out.

Firstly do some deep breathing as explained in a previous chapter.

Now relax your body. Relaxing your body means to relax your muscles as much as possible. This requires conscious effort.

Relax each part of your body. Relaxation is done first by stretching a muscle and then letting it go limp.

Start with your legs. Arch your feet upwards and let go into the limp position. Then arch your feet downwards and let go into the limp position.

Proceed immediately thereafter with the relaxation of the next part of your body. For example, after you have relaxed your feet, forget about it immediately and go on to the next part of your body.

Relax your hands. You can relax one hand at a time or relax both simultaneously. Stretch your hand upwards and let go. Then stretch your hand downwards and let go. Then clench your hands and let go. Then go quickly to the next part of the body.

Relax your back by arching it upward and letting go and allowing it to fall back on the bed.

Then relax your neck by moving it sideways from left to right, and right to left, and then up and down, finally letting it fall back on the pillow.

Then relax your facial muscles, especially your eye-brows. Contract them and relax. Frown and then relax.

Then relax your jaw. Open your mouth wide in a yawn, exhale the breath with a yawning sound and snap it into a relaxation. Then clench your teeth and let go.

Finally relax your eyes. Close your eyes and visualise black; visualising black is the best way to relax your eyes.

By this time, you may be ready to make your suggestion to your subconscious that you are feeling sleepy, feeling drowsy, and to make the rhythmic repetitions as mentioned above.

However, you may still be in an emotional state. If so, you must relax your emotions. The big emotions that affect a person are mostly worry, fear, lust, hate and the kindred ones.

You must now talk and argue to yourself quietly and silently so that you can lay aside the emotions that are assailing you at that moment. Any excitement must be allayed. You may be overjoyed at some sudden burst of good fortune. You must argue to yourself that you must go to sleep and that it is time that the excitement be allayed. You may be up against a second moment of decision to go to sleep.

Once you have reached your final moment of decision, it will not be difficult to go to sleep.

Now begin to make your suggestions to your subconscious that you are feeling sleepy and drowsy. Repeat the rhythmic repetitions:

"I am feeling
drowsier and drowsier",

OR

"Moment by Moment
And hour by hour
And I am feeling
Drowsier and drowsier".

You should soon be asleep.

Chapter 3

Auto-Suggestion

It is the Subconscious Mind that sustains and builds and repairs and heals the human body. You can aid and influence the activities by taking suggestions to your Subconscious Mind.

Your energy, your drive, your ambitions are all based on your Subconscious. You can ginger up your Subconscious by suitable suggestions.

Keep out your Will-power when making suggestions to your Subconscious. Do not make any assertions, especially an assertion of something which is not true, for your Subconscious Mind will reject an untrue suggestion. Make suggestions only, suggestions for the future.

Your suggestions are to be based on deep concentration. It is better for your suggestion to have a rhythm or lilt, so that your words do not interfere with your concentration.

The best time is when you are about to sleep. Make only one kind of suggestion on any one occasion. When you wake up during the course of the night, you can make a suggestion different to the one you made earlier in the night. Of course, you can also make a suggestion at any time of the day when your mind is at repose.

Health

Keep repeating this suggestion with a concentrated mind:
"Hour by hour and day by day,
I am getting well in every way".

For elder people who want to feel younger:
"Hour by hour and day by day,
I am getting younger in every way".

If you want to feel younger and make the above suggestion, you should in your everyday activities act younger and think younger. Throw away your old-fashioned ways of thinking and acting.

About your Work

You may be getting stale in your work. You may think that you do not like your work, or do not like it any more. However, think to yourself how by your work you are giving help to others, how others are dependent on you and your work, how they look up to you for help, the service you are rendering to others, etc.

Suggest to yourself:
"Hour by hour and day by day,
I love my work better in every way".

Success in Work

If you want success, or more success, in your work, do the requisite suggestion. Not only will there be direct results but there will also be a reflex reaction for you to be more keen on your work and to work harder.

"Hour by hour and day by day
I am more and more successful in every way".

Relations with your Spouse

You may have some difficulty with your spouse. You may think that you do not love him (her) any more, or that you love him (her) less than formerly.

147

The best cure is to talk it over openly about each other's alleged faults. If after you have talked it over with your spouse and he (she) will also make the following suggestion, the trouble will soon be over. In any case, if you do not talk it over with your spouse, at least on your part make the suggestion:

> "Hour by hour and day by day,
> I love my husband (wife) better in every way".

You may make suitable variations in the wording to meet your case.

When Doing Breathing Exercises

When doing breathing exercises, you may be doing some concentration exercise at the same time. Otherwise, you can make the following suggestion:

> "I am breathing in health".

Overcoming Difficulties

You may have difficulties for which the suggestions mentioned above are not suitable.

Then make the following suggestion:

> "Hour by hour and day by day
> my difficulties are being overcome in every way."

Pain

It has been proved that pain can be made to subside and disappear by concentrated suggestion to your Subconscious. The suggestion may have to be somewhat sustained and prolonged. It can be performed at any time when necessary. Concentrate on the spot where the pain is, and make a suggestion that the pain is disappearing.

Chapter 4

Absent-Mindedness

Absent-mindedness can be cured only by being mindful of everything from moment to moment. You must "live in the present". You must be aware of the happenings, you must be conscious of the happenings, at every moment. In due course of time, you will be conscious of each happening from the time of your awakening in the morning till the moment you fall asleep.

This awareness of every moment can be cultivated gradually till you are no more ever absent-minded. Try it for 5 minutes at first and then gradually extend the time. You will be living every moment for the first time in your life, and you will discover how interesting it really is.

Here are a few exercises:

Exercise 1. Basic Awareness

Be aware of your breathing-in, and breathing-out. Be conscious of your breathing through the nostrils, through the nose — "In" and "Out". Let your breathing be natural. Do not force the breathing.

This is to be your basic awareness throughout your waking hours. You must go back to this basic awareness of breathing-in and breathing-out as soon as you have finished being aware of whatever particular thing you have been doing, i.e. your daily chores or your daily work.

Exercise 2. Walking

Be aware of every movement of your legs. Let us say that you start walking with your left foot. First be aware of your intention to walk. Next, be aware that you move your left leg forward, then be aware that you move your right leg forward, and so on. You are aware of your walking – left, right, left, right.

Now walking more slowly, be aware of your movement of each leg in two sections or parts. Be aware of your left leg going forward and your putting it on the ground. Then be aware of the right leg going forward and your putting it on the ground.

As you improve in course of time, be aware of the movements of each leg in 3 sections or parts. Be aware of the leg being lifted from the ground, then moving forward, and then your putting it on the ground.

In any spare moment between the awareness of the movements of your legs, go back to the basic awareness of breathing-in and breathing-out.

Exercise 3. When you want to sit down on a chair

Be aware of your intention to sit down; think very quickly – "I want to sit down". Be aware of your first movement towards sitting down. When you have sat down, think very quickly – "have sat down".

Then go back to your basic awareness of breathing-in and breathing-out, till you want to do something else.

Exercise 4. When you want to get up

Be aware of your intention to get up; think very quickly – "Want to get up". Be aware of each movement towards getting up. When you are up, think very quickly – "I am up".

Before you intend doing something else, go back to your basic awareness of breathing-in and breathing-out.

Exercise 5. When you want to drink

Be aware of your intention to drink. Then be aware of your extending your hand towards the cup, be aware of pouring the water in the cup, be aware of lifting the cup towards your lips, be aware of each successive step right up to swallowing the water, be aware of putting down the cup, etc., till the act of drinking is over.

Then go back to your basic awareness of breathing-in and breathing-out.

Exercise 6. Eating

Be aware at every moment of every movement towards eating, be aware of using the fork and the knife or the spoon, of every successive movement of drinking your soup, of each successive movement of cutting your meat and putting it in your mouth and chewing and swallowing and the return movements of your hands towards your plate, and so on.

In between, go back to your basic awareness of in and out breaths.

Exercise 7. Lying down

You must always be aware of your intention to do anything; in this instance, lying down. Think very quickly – "want to lie down". Then be aware of every successive movement.

Exercise 8. The Sensations

Whatever be your physical posture, whether sitting or standing or lying down, try to be aware of your various sensations. Say you are sitting. As you sit, you will want to move your position. Think quickly "want to move". Then be aware of your movement, whatever it be.

You may feel itchy. Be aware of your itchiness. Think to yourself – "I am feeling itchy". Concentrate your mind on the itchiness. Usually, the sensation will gradually disappear as you concentrate and improve your concentration. If the sensation gets worse, you may wish to scratch. If so, think to yourself – "I am going to scratch".

Then be aware of moving your hand towards the spot, be aware of your scratching and be aware of the disappearance of the itchiness, and be aware that you have stopped scratching and that you have withdrawn your hand.

You may feel a pain. Be aware of the sensation of pain. Think to yourself — "I feel a sensation of pain". Then concentrate on the pain and make suggestion to yourself that it is disappearing and usually it will disappear. If the pain gets worse, you may prefer to change your posture to get rid of the pain. Think to yourself — "I want to change my posture". Then change it and be aware of it.

You may feel tired. One of your limbs may feel numb. There are all sorts of other sensation, of your physical body. Be aware of the sensation, be aware of your intention to do something to overcome or change the sensation, and be aware of what you do.

And always in the meantime, go back to the basic awareness of breathing-in and breathing-out.

Exercise 9. The five senses

When you see, be aware and think to yourself — "I see". Then go back to your basic awareness of breathing-in and breathing-out. Or you may wish to go on to see something else. Just be aware of whatever you are doing.

When you hear, when you taste, when you touch, when you smell, be aware and think to yourself of whatever the sensation is. Be aware, be conscious of whatever it is.

Later go back to your basic awareness of the in and out breaths.

Exercise 10. Your thoughts

Be aware of your thoughts. As your mind wanders, think to yourself — "wandering". As your mind dwells at a certain spot, think to yourself — "dwelling". If you meet a friend in your thoughts, in your imagination, think to yourself — "meeting". And so on. Then you let your imagination run riot. Be aware of every successive run of your mind. Later consciously bring your mind back and be aware of it. Be aware of every successive movement. Then bring it back to your basic in and out breathing.

Exercise 11. On reading

Be aware of your intention to read. Be aware of the opening of the book, your starting to read, and in the marginal zone of your consciousness, be aware that you are reading.

Be aware. Be aware. Be aware when you are feeling tired of reading. Be aware when you wish to stop reading. Be aware of your stoppage of the reading.

Exercise 12. On awakening

As soon as you awake, you should be conscious immediately that you are awake. This will not be easy at first. Before you go to sleep at night, suggest to yourself that you will be aware of the fact of your awakening as soon as you awake. Suggest to yourself every night before you fall asleep.

After your first moment of awareness, continue being aware of every other happening, of your movements in getting up, of your ablutions, of your walking here and there, to and fro, of your sitting down, etc. In other words, be aware of every consequential act, of taking your meals, of going to work, of your work itself and the 101 things connected with your work and your movements in their connection, etc.

Always, in the meantime, be aware of your basic breathing-in and breathing-out.

The above are a few exercises to show you the way. You can realise the immensity of the subject. Be industrious.

Try for 5 minutes at first. Then extend the time. In the end you will be aware of everything from the time you wake up till the time you fall off to sleep.

Day by day and week by week and month by month, you will improve. There will come a time when you can never ever be absent-minded again.

Chapter 5

Basic Good Conduct

Basic good Conduct is a matter of common-sense for the good of the community at large. The point is brought home by the following illustration.

To ensure harmonious relations between all the members of a community, a meeting was called and everybody attended.

A few elders of the community explained that the purpose of the meeting was to find ways and means of ensuring harmonious relations within the community and that, after due discussion, the meeting should decide what were the rules of good conduct by which all the members of the community should abide.

However, one of those present declared that he was willing to abide by every rule made by the community but unfortunately, if ever he were in a bad mood, he had a great urge, a great desire, to kill people, male or female, big or small, and that he must not be blamed if he were to kill anybody.

Another person got up and said that he had a terrific urge at times to rape women and children, and he took an inordinate delight in seducing young girls and married women. So he must be excused if he sometimes raped women and children and had sexual misconduct with young girls and married women.

Another person got up and said that he had a great urge to steal and that he must be excused if he stole other people's property directly or by way of cheating, embezzlement etc.
Another person said that he had a penchant for telling lies, especially with a view to harming the reputation of others.
Another person said that he must be excused if he got drunk off and on, and if he committed some excesses whilst he was drunk, such as assaulting people or raping women or taking property forcibly.
The meeting considered the statements of these people. Many speeches were made to the effect that everybody in the community must conform to the meeting.
Eventually the following rules were made:

1. Nobody must drink to excess or take narcotics in any form.
2. Nobody must steal the property of another by whatsoever means.
3. Nobody must tell lies especially with a view to character assassination, etc.
4. Nobody must kill.
5. Nobody must commit adultery or indulge in illicit sexual intercourse.

The meeting considered that drunkenness could lead to other offences. A person in a drunken state could kill or assault another, and commit all sorts of other excesses. Therefore, if a person must drink, he must be temperate so that no excesses are committed. As for the taking of narcotics, a person could go even to the extent of killing a person, and therefore all narcotics are banned. From the point of view of mind development, it must be realised that a few drinks can deaden or put to sleep a person's inhibitions.
Nobody wants to have his property stolen, and so everybody must respect the rights of another in respect of his property, both moveable and immoveable. You should not cheat nor embezzle nor misappropriate nor otherwise obtain the property of another illegally or illegitimately. You should avoid all dishonest dealings.

Do not lie, for lies always in the long run lead to the injury of another. You should also avoid backbiting and any other form of bringing disharmony within the community and causing enmity and hatred.

Everybody is afraid of pain; everybody is afraid of death. All animals are also afraid of pain and all animals are afraid of death; you will come to realise this if ever you hear the cries of animals that are being led to the slaughter-house. It is this common experience of suffering that unites the human and the animal kingdom. The concept of universal brotherhood emanates from this experience of common suffering. In the spirit of compassion for all sentient things, you should not kill.

Adultery has been the cause of so much trouble since the beginning of mankind, and you should nip in the bud any adulterous ideas that may start inside you. Adultery begins with the mind and has even led to wars between tribes and nations.

These rules of good conduct lead to peace and harmony in the community, but subjectively they also avoid or eliminate remorse; the benefit of non-remorse is incalculable. In the same way you should not break any of the penal laws of your country. Breaking them can lead to punishment, but most of all it leads to remorse.

In cultured societies, good conduct is based upon what "is done" and what "is not done". If you have any shame in wrong-doing and fear the consequences of wrong-doing, all is well with you. The difficulty is that many people in the community have no pangs of shame in wrong-doing nor do they have any fear of the consequences of wrong-doing.

You should cultivate a spirit of loving-kindness and a spirit of charitableness, especially charitableness towards the failings of others.

If you do any Transcendental Concentration at the end of each period of concentration you should orally offer loving-kindness to all beings in general, as mentioned in the chapter on Loving-Kindness. This has a reflex action on your own mind, and day by day builds up a snowball action.

Moreover you can, if you want, name specifically these persons, relatives or non-relatives, to whom you particularly want to extend your loving-kindness. If you were sincerely to include the names of those who you think are inimical to you or to your interest, you will be surprised how in course of time they will veer around to your side, because you yourself will react and act differently towards them.

Those without basic good conduct can still achieve good concentration but not so easily as those with basic good conduct. For those without basic good conduct, there may be a tendency to use their psychic powers for their selfish ends, and it is the common experience all over the world that such persons soon lose their psychic powers, and are even led to their physical and mental destruction.

The Superconscious Mind blossoms best in a person who lives by correct ethical conduct.

The aim of most human beings is to achieve happiness. However, the real basis of happiness is the elimination of selfish desire. Try and reduce your selfish desires as much as possible.

Let us study the following fraction:

$$\frac{\text{desires fulfilled}}{\text{sum total of desires}}$$

If for example the denominator, namely, the sum total of desires, is 100, and the numerator, namely, the desires fulfilled, is 40, you have the fraction $\frac{40}{100}$ or 40 percent fulfilled. You will still be unhappy because of desires that are not yet fulfilled.

If however you reduce the quantum of desires, if you reduce the denominator to 90, you get the fraction $\frac{40}{90}$. If you reduce your desires to 50, you have the fraction $\frac{40}{50}$, which represents the fulfilment of 80 per cent of your desires.

If you reduce your desires to 40, you get $\frac{40}{40}$ or complete happiness.

So your aim should be to reduce your selfish desires as much as possible.

Chapter 6

Self-Healing

The technique is to actively suggest to your subconscious with a concentrated mind.

When you feel that you may be catching a cold, sit down and do some hard rhythmic chest-breathing for some 20 minutes or more. Do this breathing for 3 or 4 times during the day and the onset of the cold should have abated and the cold will have disappeared.

For respiratory diseases and high blood pressure, hard or medium rhythmic chest-breathing should be resorted to. Every session should last at least 20 minutes. As you breathe you may rock your body in a to-and-fro motion. Instead of concentrating on the nose area, keep suggesting to your subconscious that your malady is disappearing. Your malady may be bronchitis, or sinus, or high blood pressure or tuberculosis or any other respiratory disease. Have two or more sessions a day. Keep at it. Others have been cured, and so can you. Do not give up, even if it takes weeks and weeks, according to the nature and intensity of the infirmity. But you will be cured.

When you are concentrating while doing rhythmic chest-breathing, you may develop aches and pains in some part of your body. After a bout of deep concentration for 20 minutes or so, transfer your concentration to your biggest ache or biggest pain and suggest to your subconscious that the ache or pain is disappearing.

After a sufficient period of concentrated suggestion, all of a sudden the ache or pain will disappear and the body and mind will feel very light. This experience should lead you to further efforts at concentration.

For the cure of other diseases such as arthritis, paralysis, gout, etc., the technique is similar to that mentioned above regarding the cessation of aches and pains. Unless you have developed very good concentration by other means, the best method is the acquisition of concentration by the chest-breathing techniques. Obtain deep concentration for 20 minutes or more, and then transfer the concentration to your infirmity, to that part of your body which is the subject of the disease and make firm suggestions to your subconscious that the disease is disappearing.

You must keep at it for days and days, and weeks and weeks. Have 2 or 3 sessions a day. The cure of your infirmity will take time; it is not to be a sudden cure but a gradual natural cure. The time taken to cure will depend naturally on the intensity of your infirmity. But the cure will really come about.

If there is a particular organ of your body or a particular part of your body that you want healed, concentrate on it as you make the suggestion to your subconscious. Otherwise concentrate on your heart as you make the suggestions to your subconscious.

Appendices

Appendix I

The 28 Properties or Material qualities of Matter or Materiality

1. The 4 **Maha-Bhuta** or 4 Primaries or 4 Great Essential Elements:
   1. The element of solidity or extension
   2. The element of fluidity or cohesion
   3. The element of heat
   4. The element of motion
2. The 6 bases or sensitive material qualities:
   5. The eye basis
   6. The ear basis
   7. The nose basis
   8. The tongue basis
   9. The body basis
   10. The heart basis
3. The 2 sexes:
   11. The male sex
   12. The female sex
4. Material Quality of life:
   13. The vital force

5. Material quality of nutrition:
    14. Edible Food
6. The 4 sense fields:
    15. Visible form
    16. Sound
    17. Odour
    18. Taste
7. Material quality of limitation:
    19. The element of Space
8. Communicating material quality:
    20. Bodily Intimation
    21. Vocal Intimation
9. The 3 Plasticities:
    22. Lightness
    23. Softness
    24. Adaptability
10. The 4 Salient features or characteristics of material qualities:
    25. Growth
    26. Continuity
    27. Decay
    28. Death

Appendix II

Fifty-two Kinds of Cetasika

Mental properties are of 52 kinds.

(a) The Seven Common Properties (**Sabba cittaka**), so called on account of being common to all classes of consciousness, viz:

1. phassa   (contact)
2. vedana   (feeling)
3. sanna   (perception)
4. cetana   (volition)
5. ekaggata   (concentration of mind)
6. jivita   (psychic life)
7. manasikara   (attention)

(b) The six Particulars (**pakinnaka**) so called because they invariably enter into composition with consciousness, viz:

1. vitakka   (initial application)
2. vicara   (sustained application)
3. viriya   (effort)
4. piti   (pleasurable interest)
5. chanda   (desire-to-do)
6. adhimokkha   (deciding)

The above thirteen kinds (a) and (b) are called Mixtures (vimissaka), or better, as rendered by Shwe Zan Aung "Unmorals", as they are common to both moral and immoral consciousness in composition.

(c) The fourteen Immorals (**papa-jati**), viz:
1. lobha (greed)
2. dosa (hate)
3. moha (dullness)
4. ditthi (error)
5. mana (conceit)
6. issa (envy)
7. macchariya (selfishness)
8. kukkucca (worry)
9. ahirika (shamelessness)
10. anottappa (recklessness)
11. uddhacca (distraction)
12. thina (sloth)
13. middha (torpor)
14. vicikiccha (perplexity)

(d) The twenty-five Morals (**kalayanajatika**) viz:
1. alobha (disinterestedness)
2. adosa (amity)
3. amoha (reason)
4. saddha (faith)
5. sati (mindfulness)
6. hiri (modesty)
7. ottappa (discretion)
8. tatramajihattata (balance of mind)
9. kayapassaddhi (composure of mental properties)
10. cittapassaddhi (composure of mind)
11. kayalahuta (buoyancy of mental properties)
12. cittalahuta (buoyancy of mind)
13. kayamuduta (pliancy of mental properties)
14. citta muduta (pliancy of mind)
15. kayakammanata (adaptability of mental properties)
16. cittakammanata (adaptability of mind)
17. kayapagunnata (proficiency of mental properties)

18. cittapagunnata (proficiency of mind)
19. kayujukata (rectitude of mental properties)
20. cittajukata (rectitude of mind)
21. sammavaca (right speech)
22. sammakammanata (right action)
23. sammaajiva (right livelihood)
(the immediately preceding three are called the Three Abstinences)
24. karuna (pity)
25. mudita (appreciation)
The last two are called the two Illimitables or Appamanna.

1. Phassa means contact, and contact means the faculty of pressing the object (arammana), so as to cause the agreeable or disagreeable sap (so to speak) to come out. So it is the main principle or prime mover of the mental properties in the uprising. If the sap cannot be squeezed out, then all objects (arammana) will be of no use.

2. Vedana means feeling, or the faculty of tasting the sapid flavour thus squeezed out by the phassa. All creatures are sunk in this vedana.

3. Sanna means perception, or the act of perceiving. All creatures become wise through this perception, if they perceive things with sufficient clearness in accordance with their own ways, custom, creed, and so forth.

4. Cetana means volition or the faculty of determining the activities of the mental concomitants so as to bring them into harmony. In the common speech of the world we are accustomed to say of one who supervises a piece of work that he is the performer or author of the work. We usually say: "Oh, this work was done by so-and-so", or "This is such and such a person's great work". It is somewhat the same in connection with the ethical aspects of things. The volition (cetana) is called the door (kamma), as it determines the activities of the mental concomitants, or supervises all the actions of body, of speech, and of mind. As every kind of prosperity in this life is

the outcome of the exertions put forth in work performed with body, with speech and with mind, so also the issues of new life or existence are the results of the volition (asynchronous volition is the name given to it in the Patthana, and it is known by the name of Kamma in the actions of body, speech and mind) performed in previous existences. Earth, water, mountains, trees, grass and so forth, are all born of Utu, the element of warmth and they may quite properly be called the children or the issue of the warmth element. So also all living creatures may be called the children or the issue of volition, or what is called Kamma-dhatu, as they are all born through Kamma.

5. Ekaggata means concentration of mind. It is also called Right Concentration (samadhi). It becomes prominent in the Jhanasamapatti, the attainment of the supernormal modes of mind called Jhana.

6. Jivita means the life of mental phenomena. It is preeminent in preserving the continuance of mental phenomena.

7. Manasikara means attention. Its function is to bring the desired object into view of consciousness.

These seven factors are called Sabbacittika, Universal Properties, as they always enter into the composition of all consciousness.

8. Vitakka means the initial application of mind. Its function is to direct the mind towards the object of research. It is also called Sankappa (aspiration), which is of two kinds, viz., Dammasankappa or Right Aspiration, Micchasankappa or Wrong Aspiration.

9. Vicara means sustained application. Its function is to concentrate upon objects.

10. Viriya means effort of mind in actions. It is of two kinds, right effort and wrong effort.

11. Piti means pleasurable interest of mind, or buoyancy of mind or the bulkiness of mind.

12. Chanda means desire-to-speak, and so forth.

13. Adhimokkha means decisions, or literally, apartness of mind for the object, that is, it is intended to connote the freedom of mind from the wavering state between the two courses; "Is it?" or "Is it not?".

These last six mental properties are not common to all classes of consciousness, but severally enter into their composition. Hence they are called Pakinnaka or Particulars. They make thirteen if they are added to the Common Properties; and both, taken together are called Vimissaka (mixtures) as they enter into composition both with moral and immoral consciousness.

14. Lobha ethically means greed, but psychically it means agglutination of mind with objects. It is sometimes called Tanha (craving), sometimes Abhijjha (covetousness) sometimes Kama (lust) and sometimes Raga (sensual passion).

15. Dosa in its ethical sense is hate, but psychically it means the violent striking of mind at the object. It has two other names i.e. Patigha (repugnance), and Byapada (ill-will).

16. Moha means dullness or lack of understanding in philosophical matters. It is also called Avijjha (nescience), Annana (not-knowing) and Adassana (not-seeing).

The above three just mentioned are called the three Akusalamula, or the three main immoral roots, as they are the sources of all immoralities.

17. Ditthi means error or wrong seeing in matters of philosophy. It takes impermanence for permanence, and non-soul for soul, and moral activities for immoral ones; or it denies that there are any results of action, and so forth.

18. Mana means conceit or wrong estimation. It wrongly imagines the name-and-form (nama-rupa) to be an "I" and estimates it as noble or ignoble according to the caste, creed, or family, and so on, to which the person belongs.

19. Issa means envy, or disapprobation, or lack of appreciation, or absence of inclination to congratualte others upon

their success in life. It also means a disposition to find fault with others.

20. Macchariya means selfishness, illiberality, or unwillingness to share with others.

21. Kukkucca means worry, anxiety, or undue anxiousness for what has been done wrongly, or for right actions that have been left undone. There are two wrongs in the world, namely, doing sinful deeds and failing to do meritorious deeds. There are also two ways of representing thus "I have done sinful acts", or "I have left undone meritorious acts, such as charity, virtue, and so forth." "A fool always invents plans after all is over", runs the saying. So worry is of two kinds, with regard to forgetfulness and with regard to viciousness, to sins of omission and sins of commission.

22. Ahirika means shamelessness. When a sinful act is about to be committed, no feeling of shame such as "I will be corrupted if I do this", or "Some people and Devas may know this of me", arises in him who is shameless.

23. Anottappa means utter recklessness as regards such consequences, as Attanuvadabhaya (fear of self-accusations like: "I have been foolish; I have done wrong", and so forth,) Paranuvadabhaya (fear of accusations by others); Dandabhaya (fear of punishments in the present life inflicted by the rulers); Apayabhaya (fear of punishments to be suffered in the realms of misery).

24. Uddhacca means distraction as regards an object.

25. Thina means slothfulness of mind; that is, the dimness of the mind's consciousness of an object.

26. Middha means slothfulness of mental properties, that is, the dimness of the faculties of each of the mental properties, such as contact, feeling and so forth.

27. Vicikiccha means perplexity, that is, not believing what ought to be believed.

The above fourteen kinds are called Papajati or akusala-dhamma, in fact, they are real immoralities.

28. Alobha means disinterestedness of mind as regards an object. It is also called Nekkhama-dhatu (element of abnegation or renunciation), and Ahabhijha (liberality).

29. Adosa, or amity, in its ethical sense means inclination of mind in the direction of its object, or purity of mind. It is also called Abyapada (peace of mind), and Metta (loving-kindness).

30. Amoha means knowing things as they are. It is also called Nana (wisdom), Panna (insight), Vijjha (knowledge), Sammaditthi (right view).

These three are called the three kalayana-mulas or the three Main Moral Roots as they are the sources of all moralities.

31. Saddha means faith in what ought to be believed. This is also called Pasada (transparence).

32. Sati means constant mindfulness in good things so as not to forget them. It is also called Dharana (retention), and Utthana (readiness).

33. Hiri means modesty which connotes hesitation in doing sinful acts through shame of being known to do them.

34. Ottappa means discretion which connotes hesitation in doing sinful deeds through fear of self-accusation, of accusation by others, or of punishments in spheres of misery (apayabhaya).

35. Tatramajjhattata is balance of mind, that is to say, that mode of mind which neither cleaves to an object nor repulses it. This is called Upekkha-brahmavihara (equanimity of the Sublime Abode) in the category of Brahmavihara; and Upekkhasambojjhanga (equanimity that pertains to the factors of Enlightenment) in the Bojjhanga.

36. Kayapassaddhi means composure of mental properties.

37. Cittapassaddhi means composure of mind. By composure it is meant that the mental properties are set at rest and become cool, as they are free from the three Immoral (Papadhamma) which cause annoyance in doing good deeds.

38. Kaya-lahuta means buoyancy of mental properties.

39. Citta-lahuta means buoyancy of mind. By buoyancy it is meant that the mental properties become light, as they are free from the Immorals which weigh against them in the doing of good deeds. It should be explained in the same manner as the rest.

40. Kaya-muduta means pliancy of mental properties.

41. Citta-muduta means pliancy of mind.

42. Kaya-kammanata means fitness of work of mental properties.

43. Citta-kammanata means the fitness of the mind for work.

44. Kaya-pagunnata means proficiency of mental properties.

45. Citta-pagunnata means proficiency of mind. Proficiency here means skilfulness.

46. Kayujukata means recitude of mental properties.

47. Cittajukata means rectitude of mind.

48. Samma-vaca means Right Speech, that is abstinence from the fourfold sinful modes of speech i.e. lying, slandering, abusive language and idle talk.

49. Sammakammanata means Right Action, that is abstinence from the threefold sinful acts, i.e. killing, stealing, and unchastity.

50. Samma-ajiva means Right Livelihood.

These three Samma-vaca, Samma-kammanata and Samma-ajiva are called the Triple Abstinences.

51. Karuna means pity, sympathy, compassion or wishing to help those who are in distress.

52. Mudita means appreciation of, or congratulation upon or delight in the success of others.

These two are respectively called Karuna-brahmavihara and mudita-brahma-vihara. They are also called Appamanna (Illimitables according to the definition "Appamanesu sattesu bhava ti Appa-manna", that is: "Appamanna is so called because it exists without limit among living beings.")

Nibbana may be classified into three kinds, viz: First Nibbana, Second Nibbana and Third Nibbana.

Freeing or deliverance from the plane of misery is the First Nibbana.

Freeing or deliverance from the plane of Kama-loka is the Second Nibbana.

Freeing or deliverance from the planes of Rupa-loka and Arupa-loka is the Third Nibbana.

Consciousness one, Mental Properties fifty-two, Nibbana one, altogether make up fifty-four Mental Phenomena. Thus the twenty-eight material phenomena and the 54 mental phenomena make up 82 ultimate things which are called Ultimate Facts. On the other hand, Self, Soul, Creature, Person and so forth, are Conventional Facts.

Appendix III

THE ABHIDHAMMA

The Abhidhamma Pitaka consists of seven treatises, namely, Dhammasangani, Vibhanga, Dhatukatha, Puggalapannatti, Kathavatthu, Yamaka and Patthana.

1. Dhammasangani — "Classification of Dhammas".
    This book has four chapters, dealing with:
    - (i) (Citta) Consciousness
    - (ii) (Rupa) Matter
    - (iii) (Nikkhepa) Summary
    - (iv) (Atthuddhara) Elucidation

    The 22 Triplets and the 100 Couplets, which comprise the quintessence of the Abhidhamma, are explained in this book.

    Three-quarters of the book is devoted to discussion of the 22 Triplets. In extent, it exceeds 104,000 letters.

    The English translation by Mrs. Rhys Davids is called "Buddhist Psychological Ethics". The main body of the book deals with the enumeration and definition of the various methods in groups of three and groups of two, by which the whole analytical teaching of the Buddha may be expressed in accordance with his different modes of analysis.

    A Commentary, something like a Vade Mecum, was written by Anuruddha Thera of Ceylon about the 8th Century, called the Abhidhammattha Sangaha. This was translated by U Shwe Zan Aung under the title, **Compendium of Philosophy**, and first published in 1910.

2. Vibhanga — The Book of Analysis.

There are eighteen Analyses in this book. The first three Analyses, which deal with Khanda (Aggregates), Ayatana (Sense-Bases) and Dhatu (Elements), are the most important.

Most of these Analyses consist of three parts — Suttanata explanation, Abhidhamma explanation, and a Catechism (Panhapucchaka).

In this treatise there are thirty-five Bhanavaras (280,000 letters).

The English translation is by U Thittila, with an Introduction by Mr. R.E. Iggleden.

3. Dhatukatha — "Discourse on Elements".

This book discusses whether Dhammas are included or not included in, associated with or dissociated from Aggregates (Khandha), Bases (Ayatana), and Dhatu (Elements).

There are fourteen chapters in this work. In extent it exceeds six Bhanavaras (48,000 letters).

The English translation is by U Narada, Mula Patthana Sayadaw (Thera), of Burma assisted by U Thein Nyun.

4. Puggalapannatti — "Designation of Individuals".

In the method of exposition this book resembles the Anguttara Nikaya of the Sutta Pitaka. Instead of dealing with various Dhammas, it deals with various types of individuals. There are ten chapters in this book. In extent it exceeds five Bhanavaras (40,000 letters).

5. Kathavatthu — "Points of Controversy".

The authorship of this treatise is ascribed to Venerable Meggalliputta Tissa Thera, who flourished in the time of King Dhammaseka. It was he who presided at the third Conference held at Pataliputra (Patna) in the 3rd century B.C. This work of his was included in the Abhidhamma Pitaka at that Conference.

This book deals with 216 controversies and is divided into 23 chapters.

6. Yamaka — "The Book of Pairs".

It is so called owing to its method of treatment. Throughout the book a question and its converse are found grouped together. For instance, the first pair of the first chapter of the book, which deals with roots, runs as follows: Are all wholesome Dhammas wholesome roots? And are all wholesome roots wholesome Dhammas?

This book is divided into ten chapters. In extent it contains 120 Bhanavaras (960,000 letters).

7. Patthana — "The Book of Causal Relations".

This is the most important and the most voluminous book of the Abhidhamma Pitaka.

The term Patthana is composed of the prefix "Pa", various, and "Thana", relation or condition (Paccaya). It is so called because it deals with the 24 modes of causal relations and the Triplets (Tika) and Couplets (Duka), already mentioned in the Dhammasangani, and which comprise the essence of the Abhidhamma Pitaka.

The importance attached to this treatise, also known as "Maha Pakarana", the Great Book, could be gauged by the words of the Atthasalini which states: "And while He contemplated the contents of the Dhammasangani, his body did not emit rays, and similarly with the contemplation of the next five books. But when coming to the Great Book, he began to contemplate the 24 universal causal relations of condition, of presentation, and so on. His omniscience certainly found its opportunity therein".

The English translation is by U Narada, Mula Patthana Sayadaw (Thera), assisted by U Thein Nyun.

Pali equivalents of English terms as they occur in the text

Page	English terms	Pali equivalents
2	Super-intellections	Abhiññās
3	conventional truth	sammuti-sacca
	ultimate truth	paramattha sacca
4	consciousness	citta
	mind or mental constituent	cetasika
	materiality	rūpa
	Nirvana	Nibbana
	colour	vanna
	smell	gandha
	taste	rasa
	nutriment	ojā
5	karma	kamma
	mind	citta
	temperature	utu
	nutriment	āhāra
6	individual essence	sabhāva
	contact	phassa
	feeling	vedanā
7	perception	saññā
	volition	cetanā
	one-pointedness of mind	ekaggata
	psychic life	jivitindriya
	attention	manasikara
	phase	khana
	concepts, ideas, notions, names, terms	paññatti

8	ultimates	paramattha
9	subject	arammanika
	object	arammana or alambana
	craving	tanhā
	1. Realm of sensuous desire	kāma-vacara or kāma loka
	2. Realm of Form	rūpa-vacara or rūpa-loka
	3. Realm of the Formless	a-rūpa vacara or a-rūpa-loka
	mental development	bhāvanā
10	Goal or Summum Bonum	Nirvana
	zen	jhāna
	purgatory	niraya
	animals	tiracchāna-yoni
	peta	petti-visaya
	ghost	asura-kāya
	human plane	manussā
	6 higher planes	deva-loka
	abode of misery	apāya-bhūmi
	fortunate sense-experience	kāma pugati-bhūmi
11	zen consciousness	jhāna
	death consciousness	cuti-citta
	rebirth-linking consciousness	patisandhi-citta
12	undercurrent subconsciousness	bhavanga
	heart-basis	hādaya-vatthu
	vision of action	kamma
	vision of an article associated with the action	kamma nimitta
	vision of the sign of destiny	gati-nimitta
13	ignorance	avijjā
14	one who has entered the Stream	sotapannā
	once-returner	sakādāgami
	non-returner	anāgāmi
	Holy One	arahat
	fetters	samyojanani

15	ordinary human being	putthujjana
	belief in a permanent personality	sakkhāya-ditthi
	doubt or scepticism	vicikiccha
	clinging to rules and rituals	silibbhataparamasa
	sensual desire	kāma-rāga
	aversion or anger	patigha
	craving for existence in the world of Pure Form	rūpa-rāga
	craving for existence in the world of Non-Form	arūpa-rāga
	pride	mana
	restlessness	uddhacca
17	attention	manasikāra
18	6 sense-Organs	
	Eye	cakkhu
	Ear	sota
	Nose	ghāna
	Tongue	jihvā
	Body	kāya
	mind-element	mano
	6 sense-objects	
	1. visible object	rūpa
	2. sound object	saddha
	3. smell object	gandha
	4. taste object	rasa
	5. tangible object	photthaba
	6. mental object	dhamma
	6 Consciousnesses	
	1. visual consciousness	cakkhu-viññāna
	2. auditory C*	sota-v*
	3. nasal C*	ghana-v*
	4. gustatory C*	jihva-v*
	5. tactile C*	kāya-v*
	6. mind C*	mano-v*
19	heart-base	hādaya-vatthu

19	1. past bhavanga	atita bhavanga
	2. vibrating bhavanga	bhavanga-calana
	3. arrest bhavanga	bhavanga-upuccheda
	4. sense-door C*	dvāra-vajjara
	5. sense-C*	panca viññāna
	6. receiving C*	sampaticchana
	7. investigating C*	santirana
	8. determining C*	vottapana
	9-15. impulsion	javana
	16-17. registering C*	tadalambana or tadarammana
20	applied thought	vitakka
	sustained thought	vicāra
	belief or determination	adhimokka
	mind-C*	mano-viññāna
	mindfulness	sati
	diligence	viriya
	wisdom	paññā
21	karma-results	vipāka
25	feeling	vedanā
	grasping or clinging	upādāna
26	birth	jāti
27	greed	lobha
	anger or hatred	dosa
	delusion	moha
	supramundane roots	lokuttara hetu
	goodwill	a-lobha
	love	a-dosa
	wisdom	a-moha
28	aggregate	khandhā
	1. matter aggregate	rūpa
	2. consciousness Agg.	viññāna
	3. feeling Agg.	vedanā
	4. perception & Memory	sannā
	5. mental formations	sankhāra
29	undercurrent subconsciousness	bhavanga

32	unwise reflection or recollection	a-yoniso manasikāra
33	Intoxicants, cankers, biases	āsava
	Into.. of sensuality	kāma-āsava
	Into.. of renewed existence	bhava-āsava
	Into.. of speculative opinion	ditthi-āsava
	Into.. of ignorance	avijjā-āsava
34	craving	tanhā
	conceit	māna
	wrong views or wrong belief	ditthi
	wrong view regarding what is not an ultimate reality	micca-ditthi
	wrong view regarding an ultimate constituent of oneself	sakkāya-ditthi
35	mental aggregates	nāma
	eternity belief	sassatha-ditthi
	conventional designations	vohara-sacca
36	consciousness	viññāna
	feeling	vedana
	perception	sanna
	mental formations	sankhāra
	craving for sense-pleasures	kāma-tanhā
	craving for existence	bhava-tanhā
	craving for self-annihilation	vibhava-tanhā
	self	atta
	impermanence	anicca
	suffering	dukkha
	no-self	anatta
	soul	atta
42	4 Primary essential qualities	mahā-bhūta
	1. manifestation of Hardness	pathavī
	2. manifestation of Cohesion	āpo
	3. manifestation of Heat	tejo
	4. manifestation of resistance to motion	vāyo

43	cells	kalāpas
	psychic life	jīvita
	sensitive parts of sense-organs	pasāda
	heart-base	hādya-vatthu
44	Impermanence	Anicca
	Suffering	Dukkha
	No-Self, No-Soul	Anatta
	all conditioned things are impermanent	sabbe sankhāra anicca
	all conditioned things are suffering	sabbe sankhāra dukkha
	all things are anatta	sabbe dhamma anatta
	nirvana	a-sankhata dhamma
45	soul or spirit	sakkhāya-ditthi
46	Law of Dependent Origination	Paticca-Samuppāda
	things as they really are	yathā-bhūta
	activity	karma
	volition	cetanā
52	craving for sensual craving	kāma-tanhā
	craving for eternal existence	bhava-tanhā
	craving for self-annihilation	vibhava-tanhā
	fine-material	rūpa
	immaterial existence	a-rūpa-bhava
	eternity belief	sassata-ditthi
	annihilation belief	vibhava or ucceda-ditthi
53	Table of Dependent Origination	Paticca Samuppāda
54	Birth or Rebirth	Jāti
57	It's my fault	mea culpa (Latin)
61	Truth of Suffering	Dukkha Sacca
	Cause of Suffering	Samūdaya Sacca
	Cessation of Suffering	Nirodha Sacca
	Path leading to cessation of Suffering	Magga Sacca
	Insight Consciousness	Vipassanā citta
	change of lineage	gotrabhu stage

63	Higher Morality	Adhi-Sīla
	Higher Mentality	Adhi-citta
	Higher Wisdom	Adhi-paññā
	Path Wisdom	Magga-Ñāna
64	Right Understanding	Samma-ditthi
66	charity	dāna
	precepts, morality	sīla
	Concentration	samatha
	Eye-consciousness	cakkhu-viññāna
	Ear-C*	Sota-v *
	Mind-C*	Mano-v*
68	31 planes of existence	Samsāra
	Thought	Citta
	Mind-C*	Mano-viññāna
	Mental object	dhamma-arammana

PAST	1. Ignorance (avijja) 2. Karma Accumulations (sankhāras)	karma-Process (kamma-bhava) 5 causes: 1, 2, 8, 9, 10
PRESENT	3. Rebirth-Linking consciousness (viññāna) 4. Corporeality-Mentality (Nāma-Rūpa) 5. Six Bases (Āyatana) 6. Impression (Phassa) 7. Feeling (Vedanā)	Rebirth-Process (Upatti-bhava) 5 results: 3-7
PRESENT	8. Craving (Tanhā) 9. Clinging (Upādanā) 10. Process of Becoming (Bhava)	Karma-Process (kamma-bhava) 5 causes: 1, 2, 8, 9, 10
FUTURE	11. Rebirth (Jāti) 12. Old Age and Death (Jarā-Marana)	Rebirth-Process (Upatti-bhava) 5 results: 3-7

Index

Note: The Pali terms appearing in this Index refer to their English equivalents on the pages indicated. For Pali terms and their English equivalents, see Pages 174-180.

Abhidhamma, 171
Abhiñña, 6
Adhi-citta, 67
Adhi-paññā, 67
Adhi-sīla, 67
Adhi-nava, 87
Absent-Mindedness, 149
5-Aggregates, 32
Ahāra, 83
Ahosi-karma, 25
Anāgāmi, 18
Anatta, 40, 48, 70
Anā-pana, 117
Anicca, 48, 70
Anuloma, 88
Arūpa, 106
Arahat, 18
Arammanika, 13
Arammana, 13
 = alambana
Ariyā-puggala, 19
Atta, 40
Attasalini, 25
Auto-Suggestion, 146
Attention, 11, 24
Ayoniso-manasikāra, 36

Bala, 65, 77
Basic Good Conduct, 154
Bhanga, 86
Big Magician, 33, 39
Bhaya, 86
Blind Man, 99
Brahma-Vihāras, 116
Body, 82
Breathing, 117, 137
Buddhagosha, 25
Buddhist Dictionary, 34

Called a car, 45
Calm, 85
Causal Aggregates, 59
Causal Suffering, 59
Categories of ultimate
 realities, 8
Cells, 47
Cetasika, 8, 162
Changeability, 46
Chromosomes, 28, 102
Citta, 72
Clinging, 29
Colour, 8, 80
Compendium of
 Philosophy, 45
Concentration, 70, 96
Concepts, 11
Consciousness, 8, 12, 18, 21,
 22, 30, 31, 101
Contact, 10, 164
Control, 50, 69
Conventional Truth, 11
Course of Cognition, 11, 16, 23
Craving, 13, 29, 38, 56, 57
Compassion, 116
Cripple, 99

Death & Rebirth, 15
Decad, 48
Dependent Genesis, 26
Dependent Origination, 26
Descartes, 73
DNA, 28, 102
Dukkha, 40, 48, 70

181

Einstein, 107
Eternity Belief, 39
Evanescent, 35

Feeling, 10, 40
Feminity, 82
Fetters, 19
First Sermon, 28
Flash Forth, 35
Forced Chest Breathing, 137
Fourth Noble Truth, 66

Genes, 28
Generators of Matter, 9
Germinal Force, 72
Goal, 14, 18, 50, 77
Ghosts, 14
Grasping Aggregates, 36, 86
Gotrabhu, 65, 88

Heart-Base or hādaya-vatthu, 47
Healing Breath, 140
H_2O, 7, 71
Hindrances, 124
Human Personality, 32

Idea of 'I', 71
Ignorance, 17, 57
Impermanence, 48
Impulsions, 23
Intoxicants, 36, 37
Individual Essence, 10
Insight Consciousness, 65
I see a rose, 44

Jāti, 58
Jhāna, 83, 121, 125, 127
Jīvita, 82, 162, 165
Jogging, 139

Kalāpa, 47
kamma, 9
karuna, 116
kasina, 115
khandhas, 34, 36

Law of Dependent Origination, 26, 27
Loving Kindness, 116, 132

Magga, 89
magga-citta, 77
magga-sacca, 65, 67
maha-bhuta, 82
Manasikāra, 11
mana, 19
mara, 7
masculinity, 82
matter, 9, 12, 46, 83
mea culpa, 61
meditation, 96
metta, 116
mental aggregates, 39
mental culture, 114
mental object
 (dhamma-arammana), 72
mental fever, 65
mental suffering, 39
Mind, 9, 44, 99
Mind & matter, 42
mind consciousness, 33
mind development, 96
Middle Way, 39
Moha, 31
mudita, 116
muncitu, 87
mundane, 20

nāma, 81, 82
nāma-rūpa, 82
nibbhida, 87
nirodha sacca, 65
Nirvana, 8, 12, 48, 73
Noble Ones, 18
4 Noble Truths, 52
1st Noble Truth, 52
2nd Noble Truth, 55
3rd Noble Truth, 63
4th Noble Truth, 66
No-self, 49
Nonad, 48
Nutriment, 9, 80, 82

object, 13
octad, 9, 47
oja, 8

182

paccaya-parigaha, 83
paccaya-vekkhana, 89
paññati, 12
paramatta, 7, 8
pathavi, 80
Paticca-samuppada, 50
pati-sankha, 87
peace, 64, 73
Pe Maung Tin, 25
perception, 11
personality, 32, 51
phala, 89
planes of existence, 14, 72
preliminary concentration
  exercises, 107
Preliminaries, 5
psychic life, 11, 47
psychic powers, 93
puthujjana, 19

rasa, 8
realms, 13, 103
rebirth-linking consciousness, 15
right action, 66
right concentration, 66
right effort, 66
right livelihood, 66
right speech, 66
right thought, 66
right understanding, 66, 68
RNA, 28
roots, 31
rūpa, 80

sakadāgāmi, 18
samādhi, 121
samma-ditthi, 68
samma-sana, 84
samatha, 96, 121
samsāra, 72
samyojanani, 19
sankhāra, 48
sankharuppekha, 88
self, 38, 50, 69
sense objects, 22
sense organs, 22
self-healing, 158
6-sense organism, 29
Shwe Zan Aung, 45, 162
sign, 125
signless state, 64

sleep & insomnia, 141
smell, 80
soul, 69, 71, 72
spheres or realms, 13
sotapanna, 18
subject and object, 13
subjective mind, 18
summum-bonum, 14, 18, 50, 77
superconscious, 104
superintellections, 6
space, 48
supramundane, 20, 30, 103

taste, 8, 80
temperature, 9
thought-process, 11, 23
transcendental, 95
1st Noble Truth, 52
2nd Noble Truth, 55
3rd Noble Truth, 63
4th Noble Truth, 66
Turkish Fashion, 108

udaya-vaya nupassanā ñāna, 85
ultimates, 7, 12
unborn, unoriginated,
  uncreated, unformed, 63
universal cetasikas, 10
unwise reflection, 36
uppekkha, 116
utu, 83

vicikiccha, 19
viññāna, 42
vipassana, 77, 78, 94, 96
vision of action, 16
vision of article, 16
vision of sign of destiny, 16
volition, 11
vohara-sacca, 39

walking on water, 93, 128
warnings, 5
wisdom, 40
wrong view, 38

yathā-bhūta (as they really
  are), 50
your Mind, 96

zen, 14

183